WERE YOU EVER A CHILD?

First published 1921
This edition published by Lector House in 2024

ISBN: 978-93-6138-201-7

Lector House LLP
Registered Office: H. No. 96, Block C, Tomar Colony,
Burari, Delhi – 110084, India
info@lectorhouse.com
www.lectorhouse.com

WERE YOU EVER A CHILD?

FLOYD DELL

2024

LECTOR HOUSE LLP

WERE YOU EVER A CHILD?

BY

FLOYD DELL

SECOND EDITION, WITH A NEW PREFACE

TO
THE SCHOOL TEACHERS
OF MY CHILDHOOD
IN TOKEN OF FORGIVENESS

Preface.

This book is intended as an explanation of the new educational ideals and methods now being fostered and developed, under great difficulties, by courageous educators, in various schools for the most part outside the public school system. These schools are "experimental" in the sense that they are demonstrating upon a small scale the vast possibilities of a modern kind of education. The importance of these schools consists not so much in the advantages which they are now able to give to a few of our children, but rather in the prophetic vision they afford of all youth growing up with the same advantages.

Before that can happen, the public must discover what the new education signifies, and why the old educational system is unable to keep up with the demands of modern civilization.

This book attempts only a small part of such a tremendous task of enlightenment. But it does undertake a brief review of the educational situation in the light of our present scientific knowledge of human nature—and more especially, of the human nature of the child.

Education may be said to be, essentially, an adjustment between the child and the age in which he lives. That adjustment can be a painless and happy one; at present it is a sort of civil war. This book deals precisely with the special problems involved in the difficult process of reconciling the nature of the child with the nature of our twentieth-century machine-culture.

The method chosen in these pages for the exposition of this situation is one which many readers will consider unduly flippant, particularly in those passages which deal with the failure of the old educational system. But one might as well laugh at that failure as cry over it; for it is a ridiculous as well as a pathetic failure. The important thing is to recognize that it is a failure, and to lend a hand if we can in the creating of a better kind of education.

F. D.

Contents

Were You Ever a Child?

WERE you ever a child?. . .

I ask out of no indecent curiosity as to your past. But I wish to address only those who would naturally be interested in the subject of Education. Those who haven't been children themselves are in many respects fortunate beings; but they lack the background of bitter experience which makes this, to the rest of us, an acutely interesting theme—and they might just as well stop reading right here. I pause to allow them to put the book aside. . . .

With my remaining audience, fit though few, I feel that I can get down at once to the brass tacks of the situation. *We have all been educated*—and just look at us!

We ourselves, as products of an educational system, are sufficiently damning evidence against it. If we think of what we happily might have been, and then of what we are, we cannot but concede the total failure or the helpless inadequacy of our education to educe those possibilities of ours into actuality.

Looking back on those years upon years which we spent in school, we know that something was wrong. In this respect our adult convictions find impressive support in our earlier views on the subject. If we will remember, we did not, at the time, exactly approve of the school system. Many of us, in fact, went in for I. W. W. tactics—especially sabotage. Our favourite brand of sabotage was the "withdrawal of efficiency"—in our case a kind of instinctive passive resistance. Amiable onlookers, such as our parents or the board of education, might have thought that we were learning something all the while; but that's just where we fooled 'em! There were, of course, a few of us who really learned and remembered everything—who could state off-hand, right now, if anybody asked us, in what year Norman the Conqueror landed in England. But the trouble is that so few people ask us!

There was one bit of candour in our schooling—at its very end. They called that ending a Commencement. And so indeed we found it. Bewildered, unprepared, out of touch with the realities, we commenced then and there to learn what life is like. We found it discouraging or inspiriting in a thousand ways; but the thing which struck us at the time most forcibly was that it was in every respect quite unlike school. The values which had obtained there, did not exist outside. One could not cram for a job as if it were an examination; one could not get in the good graces of a machine as if it were a teacher; the docility which won high "marks" in school was called lack of enterprise in the business world, dulness in social life, stupidity in the realm of love. The values of real life were new and different. We had been quite carefully prepared to go on studying and attending classes and taking examinations; but the real world was not like that. It was full of adventure and agony and beauty; its politics were not in the least like the pages of the Civics Text-Book; its journalism and literature had purposes and methods undreamed of by the professor who compiled (from other text-books compiled by other professors) the English Composition Book; going on the road for a wholesale house was a geographical emprise into whose fearful darknesses even the Advanced Geography Course threw no assisting light; the economics of courtship and marriage and parenthood had somehow been overlooked by the man who Lectured upon that Subject.

Whether we had studied our lessons or not; whether we had passed our examinations triumphantly, or just got through by the skin of our teeth—what difference did it make, to us or to the world? And what to us now are those triumphs and humiliations, the failure or success of school, except a matter of occasional humorous reminiscence?

What would we think of a long and painful and expensive surgical operation of which it could be said afterward that it made not the slightest difference to the patient whether it succeeded or failed? Yet, judged by results in later life, the difference between failing and succeeding in school is merely the difference between a railroad collision and a steamboat explosion, as described by Uncle Tom:

"If you's in a railroad smash-up, why—thar yo' is! But if yo's in a steamboat bus'-up, why—whar is yo'?"

It is our task, however, to investigate this confused catastrophe, and fix the responsibility for its casualties.

I.

The Child.

EDUCATION, as popularly conceived, includes as its chief ingredients a Child, a Building, Text-Books, and a Teacher. Obviously, one of them must be to blame for its going wrong. Let us see if it is the Child. We will put him on the witness stand:

Q. Who are you?

A. I am a foreigner in a strange land.

Q. What!

A. Please, sir, that's what everybody says. Sometimes they call me a little angel; the poet Wordsworth says that I come trailing clouds of glory from Heaven which is my home. On the other hand, I am often called a little devil; and when you see the sort of things I do in the comic supplements, you will perhaps be inclined to accept that description. I really don't know which is right, but both opinions seem to agree that I am an immigrant.

Q. Speak up so that the jury can hear. Have you any friends in this country?

A. No, sir—not exactly. But there are two people, a woman and a man, natives of this land, who for some reason take an interest in me. It was they who taught me to speak the language. They also taught me many of the customs of the country, which at first I could not understand. For instance, my preoccupation with certain natural—[the rest of the sentence stricken from the record].

Q. You need not go into such matters. I fear you still have many things to learn about the customs of the country. One of them is not to allude to that side of life in public.

A. Yes, sir; so those two people tell me. I'm sure I don't see why. It seems to me a very interesting and important—

Q. That will do. Now as to those people who are looking after you: Are your relations with them agreeable?

A. Nominally, yes. But I must say that they have treated me in a very peculiar way, which has aroused in me a deep resentment. You see, at first they treated me like a king—in fact, like a Kaiser. I had only to wave my hand and they came running to know what it was I wanted. I uttered certain magic syllables in my own language, and they prostrated themselves before me, offering me gifts. When they brought the wrong gifts, I doubled up my fists and twisted my face, and gave vent to loud cries—and they became still more abject, until at last I was placated.

Q. That is what is called parental love. What then?

A. I naturally regarded them as my slaves. But presently they rebelled. One of them, of whom I had been particularly fond, commenced to make me drink milk from a bottle instead of from—

Q. Yes, yes, we understand. And you resented that?

A. I withdrew the light of my favour from her for a long time. I expressed my disappointment in her. I offered freely to pardon her delinquency if she would acknowledge her fault and resume her familiar duties. But perhaps I did not succeed in conveying my meaning clearly, for at this time I had no command of her language. At any rate, my efforts were useless. And her reprehensible conduct was only the first of a series of what seemed to me indignities and insults. I was no longer a king. I was compelled to obey my own slaves. In vain I made the old magic gestures, uttered the old talismanic commands—in vain even my doubling up of fists and twisting of face and loud outcries; the power was gone from these things. Yet not quite all the power—for my crying was at least a sort of punishment to them, and as such I often inflicted it upon them.

Q. You were a naughty child.

A. So they told me. But I only felt aggrieved at my new helplessness, and wished to recover somewhat of my old sense of power over them. But as I gradually acquired new powers I lost in part my feeling of helplessness. I also found that there were other beings like myself, and we conducted magic ceremonies together in which we transformed ourselves and our surroundings at will. These delightful enterprises were continually being interrupted by those other people, our parents, who insisted on our learning ever more and more of their own customs. They wished us to be interested in their activities, and they were pleased when we asked questions about things we did not understand. Yet there were some questions which they would not answer, or which they rebuked us for asking, or to which they returned replies that, after consultation among ourselves, we decided were fabulous. So we were compelled to form our own theories about these things. We asked, for instance—

Q. Please confine your answers to the questions. That is another matter not spoken of in public; though to be quite frank with you, public taste seems to be changing somewhat in this respect.

A. I am very glad to hear it. I would like to know—

Q. Not now, not now.—You say you have learned by this time many of the customs of the country?

A. Oh, yes, sir! I can dress myself, and wash my face (though perhaps not in a manner quite above criticism), count the change which the grocer gives me, tell the time by a clock, say "Yes, ma'am" and "Thank you"—and I am beginning to be adept in the great national game of baseball.

Q. Have you decided what you would do if you were permitted to take part in our adult activities?

A. I would like to be a truck-driver.

Q. Why?

A. Because he can whip the big horses.

Q. Do you know anything about machinery?

A. No, sir; I knew a boy who had a steam-engine, but he moved away before I got a chance to see how it worked.

Q. You spoke of truck-driving just now. Do you know where the truck-driver is going with his load?

A. No, sir.

Q. Do you know where he came from?

A. No, sir.

Q. Do you know what a factory is?

A. Yes, sir; Jim's father got three fingers cut off in a factory.

Q. Do you know where the sun rises and sets?

A. It rises in the East and sets in the West.

Q. How does it get from the West back to the East during the night?

A. It goes under the earth.

Q. How?

A. It digs a tunnel!

Q. What does it dig the tunnel with?

A. With its claws.

Q. Who was George Washington?

A. He was the Father of his country, and he never told a lie.

Q. Would you like to be a soldier?

A. Yes.

Q. If we let you take part in the government of our country, what ticket would you vote?

A. The Republican ticket. My father is a Republican.

Q. What would you do if you had ten cents?

A. I'd go to see Charley Chaplin in the moving-picture show.

Q. Thank you. You can step down.

A. Yes, sir. Where is my ten cents?

And now, gentlemen, you have heard the witness. He has told the truth—and nothing but the truth—and he would have told the whole truth if I had not been vigilant in defence of your modesty. He is, as he says, a foreigner, incompletely naturalized. In certain directions his development has proceeded rapidly. He shows a patriotism and a sense of political principles which are quite as mature as most of ours. But in other directions there is much to be desired. He does not know what kind of world it is he lives in, nor has he any knowledge of how he could best take his place, with the most satisfaction to himself and his fellow-men, in that world—whether as farmer or engineer, poet or policeman, or in the humbler but none the less necessary capacities of dustman or dramatic critic.

It would be idle for us to pretend that we think it will be easy for him to learn all this. But without this knowledge he is going to be a nuisance—not without a certain charm (indeed, I know several individuals who have remained children all their lives, and they are the most delightful of companions for an idle hour), but still, by reason of incapacity and irresponsibility, an undesirable burden upon the community: unable to support himself, and simply not to be trusted in the responsible relations of marriage and parenthood. We simply can't let him remain in his present state of ignorance.

And yet, how is he ever going to be taught? You have seen just about how far private enterprise is likely to help him. That man and woman of whom he told us have other things to do besides teach him. And if he is turned over to special private institutions, we have no guarantee that they will not take advantage of his helplessness, keep him under their control and rob him of freedom of movement for a long term of years, set him to learning a mass of fabulous or irrelevant information, instil in him a fictitious sense of its value by a system of prizes and punishments, and finally turn him out into our world no better prepared to take his proper part in it than he was before; and thus, having wasted his own time, he would have to waste ours by compelling us to teach him all over again.

In fact, the difficulty of dealing with him appears so great that I am moved to make the statesmanlike proposal—never before, I believe, presented to the public—of passing a law which will prevent this kind of undesirable immigration altogether.

Shall we abolish the Child?

The only other reasonable alternative is for us to undertake this difficult and delicate business of education ourselves—assume as a public responsibility the provision of a full opportunity for this helpless, wistful, stubborn little barbarian to find out about the world and about himself. Well, shall we do that?

Let us not allow any false sentimentality to affect our decision. . . .

The vote seems to be in favour of giving him his chance. Very well!

II.

The School Building.

IT is clear that what is most of all the matter with the child is his sense of helplessness. . . . He told us how he lost inevitably his position of King in the magic realm of infancy—a kingship only to be recovered fragmentarily in dreams and in the fantasies of play—how he discovered himself to be little and weak and clumsy and ignorant of the ways of the strange real world. It is clear too that the chief difference which separates us from childhood is the acquisition of a few powers, physical and intellectual, which make us feel to some extent masters of our world.

Does not education, then, first of all consist in giving to children a progressive sense of power, through a physical and intellectual mastery of their environment? And would not the acquisition of an adequately increasing mastership deprive the child of any need for those outbursts of rage and malice and mischief which are today the most characteristic trait of childhood, and which are only his attempt to deny his shameful helplessness? Shall we not try at the outset to make the child feel that he is a useful and important part of our world?

The answer to these questions being "Yes," we now turn to the building in which what now passes for education is conducted, and inquire whether it answers this primary requirement.

But first of all, let us free our minds from any lingering superstitions we may cherish with reference to school buildings. Let us get over the notion that school-buildings are sacrosanct, like churches. I am inclined to think that we have transferred to the school building some of our traditional respect for churches. We feel that it is a desecration to allow dances and political meetings to be held there. We seem to regard with jealous pride the utter emptiness and uselessness of our school buildings after hours; it is a kind of ceremonial wastefulness which appeals to some deep-seated ridiculous barbaric sense of religious taboo in us. Well, we must get over it if we are to give the children a square deal. If it should turn out that the school building is wrong, we must be prepared to abolish it.

And we must get over our notion that a school building is necessary in order for a school to exist. The most famous school in the world had no building at all—only a stretch of outdoors, with some grass and a few plane trees. Of course, the

Greeks were fonder of the open air than we are, and their winters were less severe. And then, too, the Greek idea of education was simpler than ours. It comprised simply athletics and philosophy and one or two other aristocratic subjects which I forget at the moment—art being regarded as manual labour, just as the drama was considered a religious function, and government a kind of communal festivity! And, of course, the Persian theory of education—to be able to ride, shoot, and tell the truth—could be carried out under the open sky better than anywhere else. But our aims are more elaborate, and it may very well be true—in fact, I have been convinced of it all along—that much of our educational process should be carried on indoors.

But let us not be too hasty in conceding the School Building's right to existence. There is another side to the question.

The trouble is, once you give a School Building permission to exist, it straightway commences to put on semi-sacerdotal airs—as if it were a kind of outcast but repentant church. It arranges itself into dingy little secular chapels, with a kind of furtive pulpit in front for the teacher, and a lot of individual pews for the mourners. It makes the chemistry laboratory, which it regards as a profane intruder, feel cramped and uncomfortable; it puts inconveniences in the way of the gymnasium; and it is dreadfully afraid some one will think that the assembly hall will look like a theatre; while as for carpentry and printing shops, ateliers for sculpture groups, and a furnace for the pottery class, it feels that it has lost caste utterly if it is forced to admit them; nor will it condescend to acknowledge such a thing as a kitchen-garden in its back yard as having any relation to itself. You can well understand that if it has these familiar adjuncts of everyday life, it will seem just like part of the ordinary world; and so it tries its hardest to keep them out, and generally succeeds pretty well.

But since what we started out to do was to teach children what the world of reality is like, it is necessary that they should be in and of the real world. And since the real world outside is not, unfortunately, fully available for educational purposes, it is necessary to provide them with the real world on a smaller scale—a world in which they can, without danger, familiarize themselves with their environment in its essential aspects—a world which is theirs to observe, touch, handle, take apart and put back together again, play with, work with, and become master of; a world in which they have no cause to feel helpless or weak or useless or unimportant; a world from which they can go into the great world outside without any abrupt transition—a world, in short, in which they can learn to be efficient and happy human beings.

The School Building, imposing upon our credulity and pretending to be too sacred for these purposes, needs to be taken down from its pedestal. It may be permitted to have a share in the education of our youth if it will but remember that it is no more important in that process than a garden, a swimming tank, a playground, the library around the corner, the woods where the botany class goes, or the sky overhead that exhibits its constellations gladly at the request of the science teacher. Let it humble itself while there is yet time, and not expect its little guests to keep silence within its walls as if they were in a church, for it may even yet be overthrown—and replaced by a combination theatre-gymnasium-studio-office-and-model-factory building. And *then* it will be sorry!

III.

The Teacher.

SHALL the Teacher be abolished?. . .

What's that you say?—Oh, but surely not before she has had a hearing!—the worst criminal deserves that much consideration. I beg of you to let me speak one moment in her behalf.—Ah, thank you, my friends.

(Sister, you had a tight squeak just then! If it hadn't been for my presence of mind and my habitual coolness in the presence of infuriated mobs, I hate to think what would have happened.—And now let me see: what *can* I say in your behalf? H'm. . . . H'm. . . .)

My friends, this unhappy woman (for we shall centre our attention on the female of the species) is more sinned against than sinning. Reflect! The status of women in the United States has changed in the last fifty years. Modern industry has almost utterly destroyed the old pioneer home with its partnership-marriage; ambitious young men no longer have an economic need for capable women-partners; women have lost their wonted economic value as potential helpers, and their capacity for motherhood appears to the largest section of young manhood in the aspect of a danger rather than a blessing. Women have, to be sure, acquired a new value, in the eyes of a smaller class of economically "arrived" men, as a sign of their "arrival"—that is, they are desired as advertisements of their husbands' economic status. In one sense, the task of demonstrating the extent of a husband's income is easier than the pioneer task of helping take care of a farm and raising a houseful of babies; but, after all, such a career does require either natural talent or a high degree of training in the graceful habits of conspicuous idleness and honorific extravagance. And, whether it is that the vast majority of women spurned such a career as an essentially immoral one, or whether they were not really up to its requirements, or whether the demand was found to be more than met by the hordes of candidates turned out yearly by the boarding-schools—whatever the reason, the fact remains that a large number of women began to see the necessity and to conceive the desirability of some career other than marriage. But industrial evolution, which had destroyed their former opportunities, had failed to make any considerable or at least any decent room for them in the industrial scheme.

Most particularly was this true for the young women of the middle class. They were unable to go into the professions or the respectable trades, and unwilling (for excellent reasons) to enter the factories; they were given no opportunity to learn how to do anything—they were (quite against their will, but inevitably) condemned to profound ignorance of the most important things in the world—work and love; and so, naturally, they became Teachers.

The world did not want them, and so they stayed out of the world, in that drab, quasi-religious edifice, the School Building, and prepared others to go into the world. . . .

Good Heavens! do you suppose for a minute, if this unfortunate woman had known enough about Anything in Particular to get a respectable job outside, that she would have stayed in there to teach Everything in General?[1] Do you suppose she *wants* to be a Teacher? Do you suppose she likes pretending to be adept in a dozen difficult subjects at once, inflicting an impossible ideal of "order" upon the forty restless children whom her weary, amateur, underpaid efforts at instruction have failed to interest, spending her days in the confronting of an impossible task and her nights in the "correcting" of an endless series of written proofs of her failure—and, on top of that, being denied most of her human rights? The munition-factory girls at least had their fling when the day's work was over; but she is expected to be a Vestal. In some places she can't get married without losing her job; in New York, if she is married, she can't have a baby! No—it is her misfortune, not her fault, that she is what she is.

In fact, I think that if we could have managed to keep the war going a little longer, she would have pretty much abolished herself. Abdication is becoming popular, and she among all the monarchs is not the least uncomfortable and restricted and hedged in by useless divinity. Her abdication will be as disturbing an event as the Russian Revolution. The Russians were accustomed to their Czar; but they just had to learn to get along without him. And perhaps a similar lesson is in store for us. . . .

You find it a little difficult to imagine what School would be like without Teachers? Well, for one thing, it would be more like the rest of the world than it is now—and that, we agreed, was what we wanted. Where else, indeed, except in School, do you find Teachers? The rest of the world manages to get along without them very well. Perhaps it is merely a superstition that they are needed in School! Let us inquire into the matter.

What do people in the outside world do when they want to learn something? They go to somebody who knows about it, and ask him. They do not go to somebody who is reputed to know about everything—except, when they are very young, to their parents: and they speedily become disillusioned about *that* variety of omniscience. They go to somebody who might reasonably be expected to know about the particular thing they are interested in. When a man buys a motor-car, he does not say to himself: "Where can I find somebody who can teach me how to run

[1] It will, I hope, be clear that these remarks apply specifically to the grammar school teacher who does have to teach everything. The case is less desperate in the higher reaches of our school system.

a motor-car and dance the tango and predict a rise on the stock-market?" He does not look in the telephone directory under T. He just gets an experienced driver to teach him. And when the driver tells him that this is the self-starter, and proceeds to start the car with it, a confidence is established which makes him inclined to believe all he can understand of what he is presently told about the mysterious functions of the carburetor. He does not even inquire if the man has taken vows of celibacy. He just pays attention and asks questions and tries to do the thing himself, until he learns.

But this case, of course, assumes an interest of the pupil in the subject, a willingness and even a desire to learn about it, a feeling that the matter is of some importance to himself. And come to think of it, these motives are generally present in the learning that goes on in the outside world. It is only in School that the pupil is expected to be unwilling to learn.

When you were a child, and passed the door of the village blacksmith shop, and looked in, day after day, you saw the blacksmith heating a piece of iron red hot in the furnace, or twisting it deftly with his pincers, or dropping it sizzling into a tub of water, or paring a horse's hoofs, or hammering in the silvery nails with swift blows; you admired his skill, and stood in awe of his strength; and if he had offered to let you blow the bellows for him and shown you how to twist a red-hot penny, that would have been a proud moment. It would also have been an educational one. But suppose there had been a new shop set up in the town, and when you looked in at the open door you saw a man at work painting a picture; and suppose a bell rang just then, and the man stopped painting right in the middle of a brush-stroke, and commenced to read aloud "How They Brought the Good News from Ghent to Aix"; and suppose when he was half way through, the bell rang again, and he said, "We will go on with that tomorrow," and commenced to chisel the surface of a piece of marble; and then, after a little, somewhat exhaustedly, started in to play "The Rock of Ages" on a flute, interrupting the tune to order you to stand up straight and not whisper to the little boy beside you. There's no doubt what you would think of him; you would know perfectly well that he was crazy; people don't do things in that way anywhere in the world, except in school. And even if he *had* assured you that painting and poetry, sculpture and music, were later in your life going to be matters of the deepest importance and interest, and that you should start in now with the determination of becoming proficient in the arts, it would not have helped much. Not very much.

It's nonsense that children do not want to learn. Everybody wants to learn. And everybody wants to teach. And the process is going on all the time. All that is necessary is to put a person who knows something—really knows it—within the curiosity-range of some one who doesn't know it: the process commences at once. It is almost irresistible. In the interest of previous engagements one has to tear one's self away from all sorts of opportunities to learn things which may never be of the slightest use but which nevertheless are alluring precisely because one does not know them.

People talk about children being hard to teach, and in the next breath deplore the facility with which they acquire the "vices." That seems strange. It takes as much patience, energy and faithful application to become proficient in a vice as it does to learn mathematics. Yet consider how much more popular poker is than equations! But did a schoolboy ever drop in on a group of teachers who had sat up all night parsing, say, a sentence in Henry James, or seeing who could draw the best map of the North Atlantic States? And when you come to think of it, it seems extremely improbable that any little boy ever learned to drink beer by seeing somebody take a tablespoonful once a day.

I think that if there were no teachers—no hastily and superficially trained Vestals who were supposed to know everything—but just ordinary human beings who knew passionately and thoroughly one thing (but you'd be surprised to find what a lot of other knowledge that would incidentally comprise!) and who had the patience to show little boys and girls how to do that thing—we might get along without Immaculate Omniscience pretty well. Of course, we'd have to pay them more, because they could get other jobs out in the larger world; and besides, you couldn't expect to get somebody who knows how to do something, for the price you are accustomed to pay those who only know how to teach everything.

Nor need the change necessarily be abrupt. It could probably be effected with considerable success by firing all the teachers at the beginning of the summer vacations, and engaging their services as human beings for the next year. Many of them would find no difficulty at all in readjusting themselves. . . .

IV.

The Book.

OF the ingredients of the educational catastrophe, the only one remaining to be discussed is the Book. Is it to blame for the failure of the process which has brought us to our present state of elaborate ignorance, and ought it to be abolished?

What have books got to do with education, anyway?

Not half as much as most people think! If education is learning to be a civilized human being, books have their place in it. But civilized life is composed of a number of things besides books—it contains machinery, art, political organization, handicraft, flowers and birds, and other things too numerous to mention, all of which are notoriously capable of being learned about in the great world outside without the use of books. If in the great world outside the school, then why not in the little world inside the school?

Not that the use of books should be ever avoided anywhere for the sake of the avoidance. Books are a convenience—or an inconvenience, as the case may be. Like other valuable human utilities, they are frequently a nuisance if obtruded in the place of better things. Every intelligent person has the same attitude toward books that he has toward his sweetheart's photograph: if she is out of reach, if the picture furnishes him his only way of seeing her, he values it profoundly; but if she is in the next room, he does not linger with the image. True, he may fall in love with the picture first—the picture may reveal to him the girl whom otherwise he might never have appreciated; and books do make us appreciate aspects of reality which we have neglected. But in education books are not an adequate substitute for direct contact with the realities with which they deal, precisely because they do not give the sense of power which only comes from direct contact with reality. It is the function of books to assist in that educational contact—not to take the place of it.

There is, indeed, a sense in which books are the most egregious fraud ever perpetrated upon a world hungry for the knowledge which *is* power. I am reminded of the scene in "The Wild Duck," when the father returns home from a grand dinner party. He has promised to bring his little daughter some sweetmeats or cake—and he has forgotten to do so. But—he grandly draws from his pocket a piece of printed matter—"Here, my child, is the menu: you can sit down and read about the whole dinner!" Poor little Hedvig knew that she wasn't getting anything to eat; but some of us don't realize that for years and years; we dutifully masticate the innutritious contents of text-books while we are starving for a taste of reality.

Take geography, for instance. I know quite well that it was not the intention of the author of the text-book which I studied that I should conceive the state of Illinois as yellow and the neighbouring state of Indiana as pale green: but I do to this day. They were not realities to me, but pictures in a book; and they were not realities because they had no relation whatever to real experience. If I had been asked to draw a map of the school grounds, with the boys' side distinguished by one colour and the girls' by another, that convention would thereafter have seemed only what it was. If I had drawn a map of the town I lived in, I would have been thenceforth unable, I am sure, to see a map without feeling the realities of stream and wood and hill and house and farm of which it is a conventional abstraction. I would, in short, have learned something about geography. The very word would have acquired a fascinating significance—the depiction of the surface of the earth! whereas all the word geography actually means to me now is—a large flat book. And if an aviator should stop me and ask which is the way to Illinois, I couldn't for my life tell him: but if you brought me that old geography book and opened it to the map of the United States, I could put my finger on Illinois in the dark! You see, Illinois is for me not a part of the real world—it is a yellow picture in a large flat book.

In the same way, I have the impression that the American Revolution happened in a certain thick book bound in red cloth—not by any chance in the New York and New England whose streets I have walked in. (And, for that matter, as I have later discovered, much of the American Revolution of the school histories—such as the Boston Tea-Party as described—did not happen anywhere except in the pages of such text-books). The only thing I know about the crossing of the Delaware, for example, is that it is a Leading Fact of American History, and occurred on the right hand page, a little below and to the left of a picture. And this conception of historical events as a series of sentences occurring in a certain order on a certain page, seems to me the inevitable consequence of learning history from a text-book.

There are other objections to the use of text-books. One is their frequent perversion or suppression of truth for moral, patriotic or sentimental reasons: in this respect they are like practically all books intended for children. They are generally pot-boilers written by men of no standing in the intellectual or even in the scholastic world. But even when a text-book is written by a man of real learning, the absence of a critical audience of his equals seems often to deprive him of a stimulus necessary to good writing, and leave him free to indulge in long-repressed childishnesses of his own which he would never dare exhibit to a mature public. And even when text-books are neither grossly incompetent nor palpably dishonest, there is nevertheless almost invariably something cheap and trashy about their composition which repels the student who can choose his own books. Why should they be inflicted upon helpless children?

Even if all text-books were miracles of accuracy and order, even if they all showed literary talent of a high degree, their usefulness would still be in question. If children are to be given a sense of the reality of the events which they study, they must get some feeling of contact with the facts. And to this project the use of a text-book is fatal. Let us turn to history once more. I take it that a text-book of history, as intended and as used, is a book which tells everything which it is believed necessary for the pupil to know. Right there it divorces itself, completely and irrevocably, from the historical category. History is *not* a statement of what people ought to know. History is an *inquiry* into the nature and relationship and significance of past events. Not a pronouncement upon these things, but a searching into them. Now the outstanding fact about past events is that they happened some time ago. The historian does not, to begin with, know what happened, let alone how and why it happened. He is dependent upon other people's reports. His chief task is often to determine the comparative accuracy of these various reports. And when we read the writings of a real historian, the sense of contact we have with the events under discussion comes from our feeling that we have listened to a crowd of contrary witnesses, and, with our author's assistance, got at the truth behind their words. More than that, the historian himself is addressing you, not as if he thought you had never read anything on the subject before and never would again, but with implicit or explicit reference to the opinions of other historians. He is himself only one of a crowd of witnesses, from all of whose testimony he expects you to form your own opinion of those past events which none of you will ever meet face to face.

Compare this with the school text-book. It was evidently written by Omniscience Itself, for it does not talk as if the facts were in the slightest doubt, as if there were any two opinions about them, as if it were necessary to inquire into the past to find out something about it. It does not condescend to offer an opinion in agreement or in controversy with the views of others. It does not confess any difficulty in arriving at a just conclusion. No—it says *This happened* and *That happened*. Perhaps it is all true as gospel. But facts so presented are abstractions, devoid of the warmth and colour of reality. Even the schools have learned how uninteresting dates are. But they do not realize that dates are uninteresting because, since nobody can possibly doubt them, it does no good whatever to believe in them. It is only those truths which need the assistance of our belief that engage our interest. It is only then that they concern us. We are interested in politics because it is the process of making up our minds about the future; and we are interested in history, when we *are* interested, because it is the process of making up our minds about the past.

By eliminating the text-book, or by using it simply as a convenient syllabus and chronological guide to an inquiry into the significance and relationship of the events of the past, with the aid of every good historical work available for reference, the study of history would become a matter of concern to the pupil; and the past, looked at from several angles, and down a felt perspective of time, would become real.

I am aware that this is done in the higher flights of the educational system. But why is it that the easy and profitable methods of learning are put off so long and the hardest and most profitless forced upon children? Is it that easier learning means harder teaching? I am not sure of that; the only difficulty about such a method as I have described would be in the mere change from the old to the new. No, I think the real trouble lies in the superstition of the Book.

This may be seen in the teaching of mathematics. Before they come to school, children have usually learned to count, and learned easily because they were counting real objects. The objective aspect of mathematics is almost immediately lost sight of in school. Even the blackboard affords no release from the book, for who ever saw a blackboard outside a schoolroom? Mathematics comes to seem something horribly useless. The child simply does *not believe* that people ever go through these tortures when they grow up. Even the suggestive fables into which the "examples" are sometimes cast, fail to convince him. "If a carpenter—" "A salesman has—" But he is neither a carpenter nor a salesman. He is a weary child, and he is not going to pretend to be a carpenter or a salesman unless he gets some fun out of it. The thing about a carpenter or a salesman which appeals to the child's imagination is something other than mathematics. No, the printed word does not suffice. But let him *be* a carpenter or salesman for the nonce, let him with saw or sugar-scoop in hand find it to be necessary to add, subtract, multiply, divide and deal in fractions, and he will rise undaunted to the occasion. And, having found in actual practice just what his difficulties are, he will cheerfully use book and blackboard. Where there's a will there's a way, and mathematics has only to come to seem a desirable acquisition to become an easily mastered one. I should say that the ideal way of teaching a boy of eight mathematics—including, if necessary, trigonometry—is as a part of the delightful task of constructing a motorcycle. I remember that I gained in twenty-four hours an insight into the mysteries of English grammar which I had failed to get in the 1200 odd lessons previously inflicted on me in school—and I gained that insight in writing my first short story. When an effect that you yourself want to achieve depends on a preposition or a fraction, then, and only then, are such things humanly worth knowing.

If you want to see the most terrific and damning criticism of text-books, open one of them which has been used by a child, and see it written there on the margins in fretful and meandering curleques, which say as plainly as the handwriting on Belshazzar's wall, "I have weighed this book in the balance and found it wanting. It does not interest me. It leaves my spirit vexed and impatient." I have estimated that the scrawl-work in a single average schoolbook, if unwound and placed end to end, would extend along the Lincoln Highway from Weehawken, N. J., to Davenport, Ia.; while the total energy which goes into the making of these scrawls each day in the public schools of New York City alone, would be sufficient to hoist a grand piano to the top of the Woolworth building. The grand total for the United States of the soul-power that dribbles out into these ugly pencilings, amounts to a huge Niagara of wasted energy.

The Book, as the centre of our educational process, must be demoted. It is a good servant, but a bad master. And only as a servant can it be tolerated—as an adjunct to the gardens and workshops and laboratories and kitchens and studios and playgrounds of the school-world.

V.

The Magic Theory of Education.

BUT these are not the only superstitions which have muddled the educational process. You have heard that favourite speech of the condemned criminal: "I never had no education."

He does not refer to moral education; he is not complaining that he was never instructed as to the sacredness of life and private property. He means that he never studied arithmetic and geography and spelling—or not enough to mention. He means that geography, etc., would have saved him from a life of crime and a finish behind the bars.

And you have heard some unlettered parent, come from a foreign shore, repeat over and over:

"My boy, *he* get education. I no have education. But my boy—he get education." Or words to that effect.

True; his boy will have a better chance than he himself had; he may become President of the United States or of a Fruit Trust. And it is equally true of the other man, that if he had learned arithmetic in school instead of sneak-thievery from the Carmine street gang, he would probably now be making shoes in a factory instead of in Sing Sing. There is much plain common sense in both these views of education. But there is more of plain folk-mysticism.

Both speakers think of themselves as having had to struggle along in the ordinary natural way, in the one case by day-labour and in the other by petty larceny; and they contrast their lot with that of the fortunate ones who by means of an esoteric kind of knowledge have found an easy way of life. This knowledge, they believe, is reposed exclusively in certain difficult and officially designated books, which can be made to yield their secrets only through a process called going-to-school, and by the aid of a kind of public functionary called a teacher.

This mysterious and beneficent procedure is the popular conception of education. The school building and the teacher are the later and more external elements of the cult. It is at heart a belief in the magic—one might call it the black-and-white magic—of books.

Now the essence of the belief in magic is the wish of the weak person to be strong—magic being the short straight line in the wish-world from weakness to strength.

Think for a moment of some childhood fairy tale. The Hero is not the strong man. It is the wicked Giant who is strong. The rôle of brute force is always played by malevolent powers. The Hero, stripped of his magical appurtenances, is not much to look at. Almost invariably he is the youngest of the family, and is often represented as diminutive in size or stature. And the older the fairy tale, the more physically insignificant he is. It is only later, when the motif of romantic love enters into folk-fiction, that the hero must be tall and handsome. At the earlier period he is frankly a weakling, as Man in primitive times no doubt felt himself to be, in comparison with the mastodon and the aurochs; and frequently he is regarded at the outset by the rest of the family with contempt, as no doubt was Man by the other animals when his great Adventure began. Like Man, the fairy-tale hero is confronted with an impossible task—sometimes by a whole series of such tasks, which he must somehow perform successfully if he wishes to survive; and, by no superior strength, but by some blessed help from outside, a singing bush, a talking bird, by the aid of some supernatural weapon, and, above all, by the use of some talismanic Word, he achieves his exploits. Thus does the weakling, the youngest child, the harassed prey of hateful powers, become the Giant-Killer, the Dragon-Slayer, the Conquering Hero!

It is very human, this pathetic assertion that weakness *must* turn into strength. And, if it had not been for such a confidence, primitive Man might very well have given up the game, surrendered the field to his contemporaries of the animal kingdom. And this confidence might, somewhat fancifully, be described as a previsionary sense in early Man of the larger destinies of his race. In very truth, the weakness from which it sprang was the thing which made possible these larger destinies. For the unlimited adaptations of mankind are due precisely to his weakness. It is because Man lacked the horns of the bull and the teeth of the tiger that he was forced to invent the club, the spear, the sword, the bow-and-arrow; it was because he lacked the fleetness of the deer that he had to tame and teach the horse to carry him; because he felt himself to be intolerably inferior to bird and fish that he could not rest content until he had invented the airplane and the submarine. In short, because he was the weakest of all the creatures on earth, he had to take refuge from the terrible truth in a childish but dynamic wish-dream of becoming—by some mysterious help from outside—the lord of creation.

Fairy lore may be read as a record of the ancient awe and gratitude of mankind to the miracles of human adaptation which served that childish wish. The all-powerful fairy wand is simply that unnatural and hence supernatural thing, the stick, broken from a magically helping tree and made to serve a human purpose; the sceptre of royalty is that same magic stick preserved to us in the lingering fairy-tale of monarchy. But more potent even than the magic of wand or sword in fairy lore is the magic of words. And truly enough it was the miracle of language which made the weakest creature on earth the strongest. *Writing*, that mysterious silent speech, holding in leash the unknown powers of the magic word until it met the initiate eye, must have had for mankind a special awe and fascination, a quality of ultimate beauty and terror. . . .

This flavour of magical potency still clings to the Book. It is the greatest of the mysterious helps by which Man makes his dream of power come true. Who can blame the poor jailbird who thinks that there was, in the dull, incompetent pages of the text-books which you and I carried so unwillingly to school, an Open Sesame to a realm of achievement beyond his unaided power to reach! And who can blame the poor immigrant parent if he regards the officially designated Books which his children bring home from school as a talisman against those harsh evils of the world which he in his ignorance has had to suffer!

But the magic theory is not the only popular superstition about education. There is another, even more deeply and stubbornly rooted in the human mind.

VI.

The Caste System of Education.

NOW what has Caste to do with Education? Quite as much as Magic. You shall see.

From the point of view of the student of education, the Caste system appears as *a method of simplifying the hereditary transmission of knowledge*—in short, as a primitive method of education. This will be the more readily apparent if we glance for a moment at its prehistoric origins.

Before man was man, he was an animal. He relied, like the rest of the animals, on a psychically easy—and lazy—mode of adaptation to reality. He had a specific set of "instinctive" reactions to familiar stimuli. Doubt had not entered his soul. He had no conflicting impulses to torment him. His bag of instinctive animal tricks sufficed.

But something happened to mar the easy perfection of his state. Some change in environmental conditions, perhaps, made his set of definite reactions inadequate. For the first time he didn't know exactly how to meet the situation. Conflicting impulses shook his mind; doubt entered his soul—and Thought was born. Man thought because he *had* to think. But he hated to, because it was the hardest thing he had ever done! He learned—unwillingly—more and more about how to live; he increased the number and the complexity of his adaptations; but he sought always to codify these adaptations into something resembling the bag of tricks which he had had to leave behind. And when it came to passing on the knowledge of these new adaptations to the younger generation—when it came, in short, to education—he did the job in as easy a way as he conscientiously could.

You have seen a cat teaching her kittens how to catch mice, or a pair of birds teaching their young ones to fly. It is so simple! The thing to be learned is easy—easy, because the cat is formed to catch mice and the bird to fly. And, once mastered, these tricks and a few others as simple constitute the sum of animal education. There is no more to learn; these equip the animal to deal successfully with reality. How a human parent must envy Tabby the simplicity and certainty of her task! She has only to go on the theory that a cat is an animal which lives by catching mice in order to fulfil her whole educational duty. And human parents did desire (as indeed, consciously or unconsciously, they do yet) such a simplification of their task. Primitive mankind wanted to pass on to the new generation a simple bag of tricks. Of course, there is no specific bag of tricks which suffices Man to live by; he is what he is precisely by virtue of a capacity for unlimited adaptation to environment. If the bag of monkey-tricks had sufficed, about all we know now would be how to climb trees and pick cocoanuts. Our ancestors learned because they must; and they passed on what they had learned to their successors—but in a form dictated by their wish to keep human behaviour as near as possible to the simple and easy character of animal life. They put on the brakes.

Because mankind already knew more than it thought one animal species ought to have to know, it started to divide itself into sub-species. The division into the male and female sub-species came first—and has lasted longest. The young men were educated for war and the chase, and the young women for domestic duties. And this is essentially a division not of physical but rather of intellectual labour. It was a separation of the burden of *knowing* how to behave in life's emergencies—a separation which by its simplicity gave such satisfaction to the primitive mind that he hated and feared any disturbance of it.

To this day a man is not so much ashamed of doing "woman's work" as of seeming to *know how* to do it. It is no disgrace for a man to sew on a button—provided he does it clumsily; and the laugh with which men and women greet each other's awkward intrusions into each other's "spheres of effort" is a reassurance to the effect that the real taboo against *knowing how* has not been violated. It is for this reason that women had so much harder a time to fight their way into the "masculine" professions to which a preliminary education was necessary than to enter the factories, where only strength was supposed to be required; and why (aside from the economic reasons) they have so much difficulty in entering trades which must be *learned* by apprenticeship. An interesting echo of this primitive taboo is to be found in New York City, where a telephone girl who wants to study the science which underlies her labours would find in certain public schools that the electricity classes are for *boys* exclusively.

The other social and economic groups into which mankind divided itself tended to perpetuate themselves as simulated sub-species by the transmission of special knowledge along strict hereditary lines. Crafts of every sort—whether metal-working or magic, architecture or agriculture, seafaring or sheep-breeding, even poetry and prostitution—came more and more to be inherited, until among some of the great ancient peoples the caste system became the foundation of society.

Ultimately the caste system *per se* was shattered by the demand of the process which we call civilization for a more variously adaptable creature—for human beings. But it survives almost intact in certain class educational institutions, such as the finishing schools for girls—institutions devoted to teaching the particular bag of tricks which will enable those who learn them to occupy successfully and without further adaptation a hereditary (or quasi-hereditary) position in society—to be a "finished" and perfect member of a definite and unchanging human sub-species.

The most potent harm which the caste theory of education has effected, however, is in its stultification of the true magic of the written word. Let us see how that came about.

VII.

The Canonization of Book-Magic.

IT was inevitable that the particular kind of knowledge which is represented by books should become the property of a certain caste; and it was inevitable that this caste should confine the hereditary transmission of that knowledge chiefly to such works as had been transmitted from the previous generation.

Fortunately, the literate caste could not extinguish literature. For the presumptively less sacred writings which had been denied entrance to the canon because they were *new* were, so to speak, allowed to lie around loose where everybody could get at them. Thus the true magic of book-knowledge was released from the boundaries of caste, and became more and more a universal property.

But nobody had any great respect for this growing body of "profane" literature. Popular awe was reserved for the body of sacred literature in the possession of the specifically literate caste. Frequently the distinction was marked by a deliberate difference in the languages or characters in which the two kinds of literature were written—sacred literature being written in the older, hieratic writing which nobody not of the literate caste could read.

Note the result at this stage of the process: it is precisely those books which are, on the whole, least likely to be of present value to mankind, which are regarded with superstitious reverence. The most striking example is found in pre-revolutionary China, where the relics of an age utterly out of touch with the newer achievements in human adaptation were learned by heart in the schools and made the basis of civil-service examinations.

At this point of our ideal but not at all fanciful sketch, a new factor enters—class jealousy. The literate caste is found to be associated and partly identified with the leisure class. Sacred literature has become leisure class literature, and the aspirations of the less fortunate classes toward leisure class prerogatives include a special desire, tinged with the old superstitious reverence, for the forbidden books. These were more or less unconsciously supposed to be, if not actually responsible for, at least bound up with, leisure class power. And finally the great democratizing movements in which some enterprising lower class wrests from some moribund leisure class its possessions, seizes triumphant hold on its "classics" and makes them a general possession.

This sketch is so pieced together from all times and places that it may decidedly seem to need the reinforcement of evidence. Let us therefore call to the stand that young man over there who looks like an Intelligent Young Immigrant. He comes unabashed, and we proceed to question him:

Q. Do you buy books?

A. Yes, of course.

Q. Admirable! You need a new pair of shoes, and yet you buy books! Well, what books do you buy?

A. Havelock Ellis, Edward Carpenter, Zola, Nietzsche—

Q. See here, you must be a Socialist!

A. Yes. What of it?

Q. What of it! Why, I'm talking about Reverence, and you haven't got any. You're not looking for the noblest utterances of mankind, you're looking for weapons with which to cut your way through the jungle of contemporary hypocrisies!

A. Of course.

Q. Well, how do you expect me to prove my theory by you? You are excused!

We'll have to try again. There's another one. Eager Young Immigrant, thirsting for the treasures locked in our English tongue. Come here, my lad.

Q. What books do *you* read? Shaw and Veblen, by any chance?

A. No, sir. I'm going to the English Literature class at the social settlement, and I'm reading the "Idylls of the King." I've read Addison's Essays and Shakespeare, and I'm going to take up the Iliad.

Q. The classics, eh?

A. Yes, sir. All the things they study at college!

Q. H'm. Ever hear of Dr. Eliot's Five-Foot Shelf?

A. Yes, sir—I own it.

Q. How much do you make a week?

A. Eighteen dollars.

Q. Thank you. That's all!

And there you are!

But please don't misunderstand me. Disparagement of the classics as such is far from being the point of my remarks! One may regard the piano as a noble instrument, and yet point out the unprecedented sale of pianos during the war as an example of the influence of class jealousy in interior decoration. For observe that it is not the intrinsic merit of book or piano which wins the regard of the class long envious of its "betters" and now able by a stroke of luck to parade its class paraphernalia; it is the stamp of caste that makes it desirable: an accordion, which merely makes music, would not serve the purpose! That boy who owns Dr. Eliot's Five-Foot Shelf does not want mere vulgar enlightenment; he wants an acquaintance with such books as have an aura of hereditary academic approval.

And it is for the same reason that Latin and Greek have so apparently fixed a place in our public education. They were part of the system of educating gentlemen's sons in England; and what was good enough to be threshed into the hides of gentlemen's sons is good enough for us!

VIII.

The Conquest of Culture in America.

THE first organized schools in America were theological seminaries. This was due to the fact that the New England colonies were theocracies, church-states. No one not a member of the church had any political rights. And the heads of the church were the heads of the state. In this special kind of class government it naturally followed that theology was the prime study of ambitious youth. But as the colonies grew more prosperous and the rule of the more godly became as a matter of fact the rule of the more rich, the theological seminaries of New England changed by degrees into more easily recognizable imitations of the great gentlemen's sons' schools in old England. Such, in particular, was the theo-aristocratic genesis of Harvard and Yale.

The gentlemen's sons' school was thus our first, and for a long time our only, educational achievement. The humble theocratic beginnings of these institutions did indeed leave a quasi-democratic tradition which made it possible for not only the sons of the well-to-do, but for the ambitious son of poor parents, to secure the knowledge of Latin and Greek necessary to fit them to exploit and rule a virgin continent. But beneath this cultural perfection, to meet the needs of the great mass of the people, there was no organized or public education whatever.[2] The result was a vast illiteracy such as still exists in many parts of the South today. The private and pitiful efforts of the lower classes to secure an education took the form of paying some old woman to teach their children "the three R's."

Of these three R's the last has a significance of its own. It is there by virtue of a realistic conviction, born of harsh experience. A man may not be able to "figure," and yet know that he is being cheated. And so far as getting along in a buying-and-selling age is concerned, 'Rithmetic has an importance even more fundamental than Readin' and 'Ritin'. Yet in the list it stands modestly last—for it is a late and vulgar intruder into sacred company. Even in a young commercial nation, the old belief in the rescuing magic of the Word still holds its place in the aspiring mind.

But why, you ask, quarrel with this wholesome reverence for books? Well—

[2] Except in *Dutch* New York, and in Massachusetts.

suppose the working class acquired such a reverence for books that it refused to believe it was being Educated unless it was being taught something out of a book! Suppose it worshipped books so much that when you offered its children flowers and stars and machinery and carpenters' tools and a cook-stove to play with in order to learn how to live—suppose it eyed you darkly and said: "Now, what are you trying to put over on me?" But that is to anticipate.

It was due to the organized effort of the working class that public education was at last provided for American children. Our free public school system came into existence in the thirties as a result of trade union agitation.[3] Its coming into existence is a great good upon which we need not dwell. But its subsequent history needs to be somewhat elucidated.

The public school system was founded firmly upon the three R's. But these were plainly not enough. It had to be enlarged to meet our needs—and to satisfy our genuine democratic pride in it. So wings were thrown out into the fields of history and geography. And then? There was still an earth-full of room for expansion. But no, it was builded up—Up! And why? The metaphor is a little troublesome, but you are to conceive, pinnacled dim in the intense inane, or suspended from heaven itself, the gentlemen's sons' school. And this was what our public school system was striving to make connections with. And lo! at last it succeeded! The structure beneath was rickety—fantastic—jerry-built—everything sacrificed to the purpose of providing a way to climb Up There; but the purpose was fulfilled.

The democratic enthusiasm which created the public school had in fact been unaccompanied by any far-seeing theory of what education ought to be. And so that splendid enthusiasm, after its initial conquest of the three R's, proceeded to a conquest of Greek and Latin and the whole traditional paraphernalia of aristocratic education. Every other purpose of public education was, for the time being lost sight of, forgotten, ignored, in the proud attempt to create a series of stairs which led straight up to the colleges. The high school became a preparatory school for college, and the courses were arranged, rearranged and deranged, with that intent. Final examinations were systematized, supervised and regulated to secure the proper penultimate degree of academic achievement—as for instance by the famous Regents' examinations. The public school lost its independence—which was worth nothing; and its opportunity—which was worth everything. It remains a monument to the caste ideal of education.

For the theory which underlay the scheme was that every American boy and girl who wanted an education should have the whole thing in bang-up style. What

[3] "The one dominant feature of this labour movement [1824-1836] was the almost fanatical insistence upon the paramount importance of education. In political platforms, in resolutions of public meetings, and in the labour press, the statement is repeated over and over, that the fundamental demand of labour is for an adequate system of education. . . .

"To this movement, more than to any other single cause, if not more than to all other causes combined, is due the common school system of the United States. . . . When the movement died out in 1835 to 1837 . . . Horace Mann was leading the 'educational revival,' and the common school was an established institution in nearly every state."—A. M. Simons: "Social Forces in American History."

was good enough for gentlemen's sons was none too good for us. That there might be no mistake about it, the states erected their own colleges, with plenty of free scholarships to rob ignorance of its last excuse. These state colleges, while furnished with various realistic and technical adjuncts, and lacking in the authentic hereditary aura of their great Eastern predecessors, were still echoes, sometimes spirited and more often forlorn, of the aristocratic tradition of centuries agone. With the reluctant addition of a kindly scheme for keeping very young children in school, the system now stretched from infancy to full manhood, and embraced—in theory—the whole educable population of the United States.

In its utter thoroughness of beneficent intention, the system was truly sublime.

The only trouble was that it didn't work.

IX.
Smith, Jones and Robinson.

AT this point there seems to be an interruption from somebody at the back of the hall.—Louder, please! What's that you say?

"I thought," says the voice, "that this was to be a *discussion* of education. It sounds to me more like a monologue. When do we get a chance to talk?"

Oh, very well! If you think you can do this thing better than I can, go ahead. Suppose *you* tell us why the American public school system failed to work!—One at a time, please. Mr.—er—Smith has the floor. He will be followed in due order by Mr. Jones and Mr. Robinson. And then I hope everybody will be satisfied. Yes, Mr. Smith?

Mr. Smith: "I am one of the so-called victims of our American public school system. I went to grammar school, to high school, and then to college. You say that is what the system is for—to lead up to college. Well, it worked in my case. My parents were poor, but I studied hard and got a free scholarship, and I worked my way through college by tending furnaces in the morning and tutoring at night. You say college is designed to impart a gentleman's sons' education. Well, I got that kind of education. And what I want to know is, what's wrong with me? I can't say I feel particularly stultified by my educational career!"

No, no, Mr. Smith, don't stop. Go right on!

Mr. Smith (continuing): "I will admit that I have sometimes wished I had taken some kind of technical course instead of the straight classical. But I didn't want to be an engineer or chemist, so why should I? In fact I didn't know exactly *what* I wanted to be. . . . I suppose my education might not unreasonably have been expected to help me understand myself better. And I confess that when I came out into the world with my A.B. I did feel a bit helpless. But I managed to find a place for myself, and I get along very well. I can't say that I make any definite use of my college education, but I rather think it's been an advantage."

Thank you for being so explicit. Mr. Jones next. Mr. Jones, you have just heard Mr. Smith's splendid testimonial to the value of a college education—how it has unlocked for him the ages' accumulated wealth of literature, of science, of art—

how it has put him in vivid touch with the world in which he lives—how it has made him realize his own powers, and given him a serene confidence in his ability to use them wisely—how fully it has equipped him to live in this complex and difficult age—in a word, how it has helped him to become all that a twentieth century American citizen should be! Have you, Mr. Jones, anything to add to his account of these benefits?

Mr. Jones: "Your coarse sarcasm, if aimed at me, is misdirected. I never went to college. I didn't want to tend furnaces, so when I finished high school I got a job. But there's something to this gentleman's sons' stuff. I had four years' start of Smith, but I feel that he's got a certain advantage over me just because he *is* a college man. Now why is that, I'd like to know? I could have gone to college too, if I had cared enough about it. But studying didn't interest me. I was bored with high school."

Exactly, Mr. Jones. And some hundreds of thousands of others were also so bored with high school that even the prestige which a college education confers, could not tempt them to further meaningless efforts. You have explained a large part of the breakdown of our public school system. In theory—but Mr. Robinson wishes to speak.

Mr. Robinson: "Theory—theory—theory! I think it's about time a few facts were injected into this alleged discussion! The fact I'm interested in is just this: I quit school when I was twelve years old. I had just finished grammar school. I *couldn't* go to high school. I *had* to go to work. What have your theories of education got to do with me?"

Everything, Mr. Robinson! You smashed one theory to pieces, you were about to be condemned to a peculiar kind of slavery by another theory, and you were rescued after a fashion by a third theory. You are, to begin with, the rock upon which the good ship Education foundered. As I was about to say when I was interrupted: the grandiose ideal of a gentleman's sons' education for every American boy failed—because there were some millions of American boys like you who *could not* go to college, and some hundreds of thousands of others like Mr. Jones here, who *would not*—who did not feel that it was worth the necessary effort. And these vast hordes of you going out into the world at the age of twelve to sixteen with only the precarious beginning of a leisure class culture, became the educational problem which the last generation has been trying to solve.

X.

Employer vs. Trade Unionist.

IT was the American Business Man who proposed the first "practical" reform; and if you have any doubt of the validity of the Caste theory, note what happened. The American Business Man knew that these millions of youths were going to enter his shops and factories; they were not going to be members of a leisure class, they were going to be wage-slaves; and so he proposed to educate them to be efficient wage-slaves.

And he might have succeeded in imposing his capitalistic version of the Caste theory of education upon our public schools, had it not been for the trade unions, who perceived in these capitalist plans a means of breaking down their own apprentice system. "What! turn the schools into training-schools for strikebreakers? No!" they said—and they bitterly opposed every attempt to introduce industrial training into the schools, and mustered to their aid the old notions of the Magic of Books. "Let the children have an *education*"—meaning book-learning; "it will be time enough for them to learn to *work* when they leave school," was the general verdict. And so in this clash of economic interests, one theory warred with another, and the theory of Education as a mysterious communion with the Magic of Books happily won.

Happily—for though the controversy had its unfortunate results, in the fixing of a prejudice in the minds of the working people against industrial education, we should not fail to realize that in that controversy the trade unions were right. We do not want to educate the children of the poor in this twentieth century to be a human sub-species; it would be better to give them fragments of a leisure class education than fix them into the wage-slave mould; it would be better that they learned Greek and Latin (or, for that matter, Sanscrit!) than merely a trade. It would be better to turn them out as they came in, helpless and ignorant, than to make them into efficient machines.

But such a choice is not necessary. It is possible to have an education which produces human beings who are neither out of touch with their age nor hopelessly confined within it—a generation which will be the masters and not the slaves of its environment.

The outlines of such an educational system were already being drawn, in theory and even experimentally in fact. But these radical proposals threatened to cost more money than governments are accustomed to expend on peaceful and constructive enterprises. Yet something had to be done in response to a popular sense of the imperfections of our system.

Something was done accordingly.

XI.
The Goose-Step.

BEAR in mind that the necessities of the case required something which would not cost any money, which would leave the system really intact, and yet which would impress beholders with the fact of Progress.

The device which answered to this description was copied from Prussia and informed with the essence of the Prussian spirit—a quasi-military Uniformity. There is nothing, indeed, so impressive to the observer as the sight of everybody doing exactly the same thing at the same time. And when that thing is totally unnecessary and very difficult, the effect is to stun the mind into a bewildered admiration. Hence the preposterously military aspect of the schools of yesterday—the marching in line out to recess and back again. Hence the drillmaster airs of the teaching force—as, for instance, the New York teacher who boasted, "I said to my pupils, 'All who live on Blank street raise their hands,' and then I turned to talk to the superintendent, forgetting to say 'Hands down'—and five minutes later, when I looked around, those Blank street children still had their hands up. That's what I call discipline!" And hence the reprimand to the other New York teacher because, when she came back from a visit to Italy, she told the geography class about her journey and passed around picture postcards, instead of hearing the children recite the appointed Lesson from the appointed Book at the appointed Hour. Think how it sounds for a city superintendent to be able to pull out his watch and say to a visitor: "At this moment every sixth grade pupil, in every school in the whole city, is opening his geography!" That is System, and it must not be deranged in order to *interest* a mere roomful of children in the realities of geography for half an hour!

I experienced some of the benefits of the Goose-Step System myself, back in Illinois—and I know just how a child feels about it. He feels just as you would feel if at the conclusion of a theatrical performance you were commanded to "Rise! Turn! Pass!" He feels humiliated and ridiculous. He feels that he is being made a fool of. The Goose-Step System is not intended to make its little victims feel happy; it is only intended to impress beholders with the fact of Progress.

And this kind of Systematization, this fake reform, has been the only serious contribution to American educational practice in the public schools during the life of the generation to which you and I belong—until within the last few years.

Fortunately, another crisis arose. In every large city the attendance at the public schools outgrew the school capacities, and it became necessary to put many children on a "half-time" basis. And this scandal demanded relief. It still demands relief. And at present we are faced with a choice between two methods of relief.

One method is familiar—to turn the grammar schools into adjuncts of capitalist shops and factories. It is the system now approved by the educational authorities of most of the large cities, including New York. The other is a sane and democratic proposal for education on scientific principles, for the benefit of the child and of the race.

XII.

The Gary Plan.

IT was in the nature of a happy accident that this sane and democratic proposal came before the public as a practical alternative to the scheme of turning the grammar schools into adjuncts of capitalist shops and factories.

It happened that a man named Wirt solved in the schools of Gary, Indiana, the problem of accommodating two pupils with a desk built for one. He did this by the simple means of abolishing the private and exclusive character of the desks. By having one-half the pupils come a little later and leave a little later than the other half, and use the desks which the others had just vacated for the gymnasium or workshop or assembly room, it was found that there were desks enough for all. And because this plan made it unnecessary to spend some millions of dollars on new school-buildings, he was invited to come to New York and put his plan in practice there.

If that had been all there was to the Gary system, it might have been adopted peacefully enough. But the Gary system was a real and hence a revolutionary kind of education, and so it met with immediate and bitter hostility.

It made the child and his needs the center of the whole process of education. It undertook to give him a chance to learn how to live. It made the school to a large extent a replica of the world outside. It gave him machinery and gardens and printing presses to play with and learn from. And right there it aroused the suspicions of working class parents, who were afraid their children were not going to get enough Book-learning. It demanded something of teachers besides routine and discipline and stoic patience; and though they came with experience to be its most enthusiastic advocates, they were in prospect roused to angry opposition. It abolished the semi-sacerdotal dignities of the school-building, and thus offended a deep-lying superstitious reverence in a public which regarded education as something set apart from life. It clashed with the bureaucratic fads of the higher educational authorities, and provoked them to financial sabotage. And finally it was dragged into politics, where as the pet project of an administration of bureaucratic reform officials it was held up to popular scorn.

But the ideal of education which was implicit in the Gary plan is still up for judgment.

XIII.
Learning to Work.

HERE, then, is the situation as it stands. Our education is out of relation to the time in which we live. It is breaking down under the pressure of economic forces which demands that it turn out people who do not have to be *re-educated* by modern industry. It cannot remain as it is. It will either be made the instrument of a democratic culture which accepts the present but foresees the future; or it will fall into the hands of those who are planning to make it a training school for wage-slaves. Here is the latter program, as described by the superintendent of schools in a great American city:

"Three years ago the elimination of pupils from the upper grades of our elementary schools and the demands of industry led us to experiment with industrial education in the grades. . . . Our controlling idea was that adolescent boys and girls standing on the threshold of industrial life should be grouped in prevocational schools in which they would receive, in addition to instruction in formal subjects, such instruction and training in constructive activities as would develop aptitudes and abilities of distinct economic value. At present the opportunity to *rotate term by term through various shops* is afforded in seven schools to approximately 3,000 boys and girls in the 7th, 8th and 9th years."

Between these two programs you must choose. Either efficient democratic education, or efficient capitalistic education.

"But," asks some one, "what is there to choose between them? Democratic education and capitalistic education both seem to me to consist in turning the school into a workshop."

Not at all! The democratic plan is rather to turn the workshop into a school. That may seem like a large order, but I may as well confess to you at once that the democratic scheme proposes ultimately to bring the whole of industry within the scope of the educational system: nothing less! But the benevolent assimilation of industry by education in the interest of human progress and happiness, is one thing; and the swallowing of the public school system by industry in the interest of the employing class, is quite another.

For the present, however, democratic education merely brings the workshop into the school, so that the processes of industry may be the more readily mastered; while capitalist education merely sends the school-child into its workshops, in order that he may become more effectively exploitable. The difference should be sufficiently obvious: in the school-workshops of capitalism the child is taught how to work for somebody else, how to conduct mechanical operations in an industrial process over which he has no control; in the democratic workshops of the school he learns to use those processes to serve his own creative wishes. In the one he is taught to be a wage-slave—and bear in mind that this refers to the children of the poor—for the rich have their own private schools for their own children. In the other, the child learns to be a free man.

That is just what irritates the capitalist reformers of our public school system. Since the children of the poor are going to be factory hands, what is the use of their having learned to be free men? They might as well have learned Greek and Latin, for all the use it is going to be to them!

And that is why you must exercise your choice. The merits are not quite all on one side of the question. There are disadvantages in the democratic plan of education. These disadvantages have nowhere been made more clear than by H. G. Wells in his fantastic scientific parable, "The First Men in the Moon." You will remember that his explorers visited the Moon in a queer sort of air-craft, and found there a people with institutions quite unlike our own. They too, however, had classes, and they had solved the problem of the education of these classes in a forthright manner which is utterly unlike our timid human compromises. One of the visitors from Earth thus describes the Lunar System:

"In the Moon . . . every citizen knows his place. He is born to that place, and the elaborate discipline of training and education and surgery he undergoes fits him at last so completely to it that he has neither ideas nor organs for any purpose beyond it. 'Why should he?' Phi-oo would ask. If, for example, a Selenite is destined to be a mathematician, his teachers and trainers set out at once to that end. They check the incipient disposition to other pursuits, they encourage his mathematical bias with a perfect physiological skill. His brain grows, or at least the mathematical faculties of his brain grow, and the rest of him only so much as is necessary to sustain this essential part of him. At last, save for rest and food, his one delight lies in the exercise and display of his faculty, his one interest in its application, his sole society with other specialists in his own line. His brain grows continually larger, at least so far as the portions engaging in mathematics are concerned; they bulge ever larger and seem to suck all life and vigour from the rest of his frame; his limbs shrivel, his heart and digestive organs diminish, his insect face is hidden under its bulging contours. His voice becomes a mere stridulation for the stating of formulae; he seems dead to all but properly enunciated problems. . . . And so he attains his end. . . .

"The bulk of these insects, however, . . . are, I gather, of the operative [working] class. 'Machine hands,' indeed, some of these are in actual nature—it is no figure of speech; the single tentacle of the mooncalf-herdsman is profoundly modified for clawing, lifting, guiding, the rest of them no more than necessary subordinate appendages to these important parts . . . others again have flat feet for treadles, with ankylosed joints; and others—who I have been told are glass-blowers—seem mere lung-bellows. But every one of these common Selenites I have seen at work is exquisitely adapted to the social need it meets. . . .

"The making of these various sorts of operatives must be a very curious and interesting process. . . . Quite recently I came upon a number of young Selenites confined in jars from which only the fore limbs protruded, who were being compressed to become machine minders of a special sort. The extended 'hand' in this highly developed system of technical education is stimulated by irritants and nourished by injections, while the rest of the body is starved. Phi-oo, unless I misunderstood him, explained that in the earlier stages these queer little creatures are apt to display signs of suffering in their various cramped situations, but they easily become indurated to their lot; and he took me on to where a number of flexible-limbed messengers were being drawn out and broken in. It is quite unreasonable, I know, but such glimpses of the educational methods of these beings affect me disagreeably. I hope, however, that may pass off, and I may be able to see more of this aspect of their wonderful social order. That wretched looking hand-tentacle sticking out of its jar seemed to have a sort of limp appeal for lost possibilities; it haunts me still, although, of course, it is really in the end a far more humane proceeding than our earthly method of leaving children to grow into human beings and then making machines of them."

The Lunar system has indeed much to be said for it; and the capitalist plan of wage-slave education has at least the merit of being a definite step in that direction.

XIV.

Learning to Play.

"BUT in either case," exclaims an indignant mother, "the child ceases to be a child—under either the democratic or the capitalistic plan—"

No, madam! The object of a genuine democratic education is to enable him to remain always a child.

"Then," says another interlocutor, "I must have misunderstood you. I thought you conceived of education as *growing-up*."

Growing up, yes—out of the helplessness, the fear, the misery of childhood, which come only from weakness and ignorance: growing up into knowledge and power.

"But putting aside forever his toys and games," protests the mother. "Forgetting how to play!"

No, madam. Learning rather to take realities for his toys, and entering blithely into the fascinating and delightful game of life. Forget how to play? That is what he is condemned to now. It is a pity. And that is precisely what we want to change.

"By setting him to work?"

What! are we to quibble over words? Tell me, then, what is the difference between work and play?

Or rather, to shorten the argument, let me tell you. Play is effort which embodies one's own creative wishes, one's own dreams. Work is any kind of effort which fails to embody such wishes and such dreams. . . . When you were first married, and began to keep house—under difficulties, it may be—was that work or play, madam? Do not be afraid of being sentimental—we are among friends. Is it not true that at first, while it was a part of the dream of companionship, while it seemed to you to be making that dream come true, it was play—no matter how much effort it took? And is it not true that when it came to seem to you merely something that had to be done, it was work, no matter how easily performed?—And you, my friend, who built a little house in the country with your own hands for pleasure, and worked far beyond union hours in doing it—was not that play?

It was *your own house,* you say. Just so; and it is the child's own house, that cave in the woods which he toils so cheerfully to create. And it was their own house, the cathedral which the artisans and craftsmen of the middle ages created so joyously—the realization of a collective wish to which the creative fancy of every worker might make its private contribution.

You know, do you not, why we cannot build cathedrals now? Because craftsmen are no longer children at play—that is to say, no longer free men. They toil at something which is no affair of theirs, because they must. They have become the more or less unwilling slaves of a system of machine production, which they have not yet gained the knowledge and power to take and use to serve their own creative dreams.

But men do not like to work; they like to play. They want to be the masters and not the slaves of the machine-system. That is why they have struggled so fiercely to climb out of the class of slaves into the class of masters; it has been that hope which has sustained them in what would otherwise have seemed an intolerable condition. And that is why, as such a hope goes glimmering, they join together to wrest from their employers some control over the conditions under which they work; and also why their employers so often prefer to lose money in strikes rather than concede such control—for the sense of mastery is dearer even than profits. That is, incidentally, why so many workers prefer a white collar job to a decent union wage—because it permits them to fancy themselves a part of the master class. And finally, that is why the industrial system is now at the point of breakdown—because a class of workers who have no sense of mastery over their jobs cannot and will not take enough interest in their work to meet the new and stupendous demands upon production. When pressure is put upon them, they revolt—and hell is raised, but not the production-rate.

Every production manager knows that even our most efficient industries are producing far less than their maximum; and he knows why. The psychology of slavery does not make for efficiency. There was a time when inefficiency didn't matter—when infants in agony from lack of sleep and girls terrorized by brutal foremen could produce more than could be sold, and were preferable to workers who had to be bargained with. Capitalism denied the worker the right to dare to think his job his own. But the wiseacres of capitalism now encourage the worker to believe his interests identical with those of his employer; they take out some of his wages and give it back to him in a separate envelope and call it "profit-sharing." But the production manager knows that such a mess of doubtful pottage will scarcely take the place of their birthright. He knows that he has got out of the workers the utmost that their slave psychology will permit. He knows that there is no use to go on telling them that the business is their affair. He knows that the only thing left to be done is to make it their affair—to put into their collective control not only wages and hours, but what they create and how they create it. The job must be theirs before they can put into it the energy of free men. Their creative wish alone can bring production to its maximum. But that is not what he is paid to do. He, too, is denied the right to shape industry to his dream; he may not make it efficient; he must try to make it more profitable. He, too, is a slave . . . a slave who wishes his master would set him free to play for a while with this great beautiful toy. He would show us how to increase production by 100 per cent on four hours work a day. He would show us how work could be made a joy to everybody. He would—but what is the use? He sits and looks out the window and wishes that something would happen. Perhaps these young men and women who have learned to play with machinery, who know it as a splendid toy and not as a hateful tyrant, who want to use it to make themselves and the world happier—perhaps a generation of such workers, the products of a democratic and efficient educational system, will have the knowledge and the power to take and use this machinery to serve their own creative dream of a useful and happy new society. . . .

Madam, have I answered your question?

XV.

First and Last Things.

"BUT is there nothing in the world of any importance except machinery?"

Thank you for reminding me! We are all inclined to be too much preoccupied with the importance of machinery. I confess that I have been so ever since, as a child, I took my father's watch apart and found myself unable to cope with the problem of putting it back together again. But note for a moment the pragmatic significance of such an infantile predicament. Of what use would it have been for some infinitely wise person to say to me: "Child, do not attach so much importance to those wheels and springs! They are interesting, in a way; but how much less interesting than the birds, the flowers and the stars!"—what good, I ask you, would such counsel have been to me at that moment? I wanted to get that watch put back together before something terrible happened to me. And mankind as a whole seems to me to be in much the same situation. For the best of reasons, it *has* to master the problem presented by a machine civilization—lest something terrible happen. Its preoccupation is born of fear. The flowers and stars (it thinks) can wait: they are not so dangerous.

And yet the infinitely wise person would have been right. Machinery must be ranked among (so to speak) the minor poetry of the universe. The astronomic epic, the botanical lyric, the biological drama, are, from any point of view not prejudiced by our fears, more important. It is only because we are so acutely conscious, all of us, of the failure of our educational system in the matter of preparing us to exist unbewilderedly in the midst of a machine civilization, that I have put such emphasis on the adequacy of the new education in dealing with that problem. It is of importance only as food is important to a starving man—merely so. And if you have heard enough about the place of machinery in education—

I see that you have. Very well, then we will go on to the matters of real importance.

What are they?

(My rhetorical questions, it seems, are always being taken literally! I was about to tell you myself, but I suppose we shall have to listen to that elderly gentleman over there, who evidently has the answer ready.) Very well, sir. What *are* they?

"I am glad to hear that you have disposed at last of the crassly materialistic aspect of your theme, and are about to deal with its spiritual aspects. For these are naturally its more important aspects. And if you ask me to specify more particularly what these are, I can only reply in old-fashioned language, and say that the important things in life, and hence in education, are Beauty, Truth and Goodness. I trust that you agree with me?"

Certainly, sir. Beauty and Truth and Goodness—or, if you will permit me to translate these eighteenth century abstractions into our contemporary terminology—the cultivation of the creative faculties, of disinterested curiosity, and of personal relationships, undoubtedly constitute the chief ends of democratic cultural endeavor. These, indeed, together with what you would call Usefulness and what we would call technical efficiency, comprise pretty much of the whole of existence. Not all of it—but quite enough to take as the subject of our new inquiry.

How can education encourage and develop, not in a few individuals, but in the masses of the people, the creative faculties which are the source of beauty?—for it must conceive its task in these broad terms if it is to be a democratic education. How can it foster in these same masses that rare growth, disinterested curiosity, from which come the fruits of philosophy and science? And how can education deal effectively with the dangerous emotions of personal relationship?

The task seems at first glance so difficult that it will be well for us to ask at the outset whether it can be accomplished at all!

XVI.

The Child as Artist.

IN this matter, most decidedly, we need expert advice. Let us start with Beauty. The one who best understands Beauty is undoubtedly the Artist. Let us call in the Artist. . . . Will you question him, or shall I? You prefer to do it yourself, I see. Very well, then—but please try to get to the point as soon as possible!

THE QUESTIONER. What we want to know is this: is it possible to teach the child to become an artist?

THE ARTIST. He is an artist already.

THE QUESTIONER. What do you mean!

THE ARTIST. Just what I say. The child is an artist; and the artist is always a child. The greatest periods of art have always been those in which artists had the direct, naïve, unspoiled vision of the child. The aim of our best artists today is to recover that vision. They are trying to see the world as children see it, and to record their vision of it as a child would do. Have you ever looked at children's drawings—not the sort of things they are taught to do by mistaken and mischievous adults, but the pictures that are the natural expressions of their creative impulses? And haven't you observed that modern paintings are coming to be more and more like such pictures?

THE QUESTIONER. Well—er, yes, I had noticed something of the kind! But is that sort of thing necessarily art? I mean—well, I don't want to attempt to argue with you on a subject in which you are an expert, but—

THE ARTIST. Oh, that's all right! The modern artist is ready to discuss art with anybody—the more ignorant of the subject, the better! You see, we want art to cease to be the possession of a caste—we want it to belong to everybody. As a member of the human race, your opinions are important to us.

THE QUESTIONER. That is very kind of you. I fear it is rather in the nature of a digression, but, since I may ask without fear of seeming presumptuous,—*are* those horrid misshapen green nudes of Matisse, and those cubical blocks of paint by I-forget-his-name, and all that sort of thing—are they your notion of what art should be?

The Artist. Mine? Oh, not at all! They are merely two out of a thousand contemporary attempts to recover the naïve childlike vision of which I spoke. If you will compare them with a child's drawing, or with a picture by a Navajo Indian, or with the sketch of an aurochs traced on the wall of his cave by one of our remote ancestors, you will note an essential difference. Those artists were not trying to be naïve and childlike; they *were* naïve and childlike. The chief merit of our modern efforts, in my personal opinion, is in their quality as a challenge to traditional and mistaken notions of what art should be—an advertisement, startling enough, and sometimes maliciously startling, of the artist's belief that he has the right to be first of all an artist.

The Questioner. Now we are coming to the point. What *is* an artist?

The Artist. I told you, a child. And by that, I mean one who *plays* with his materials—not one who performs a set and perhaps useful task with them. A creator—

The Questioner. But a creator of what? Not of Beauty, by any chance?

The Artist. Incidentally of Beauty.

The Questioner. There we seem to disagree. If those horrid pictures—

The Artist. Suppose *you* tell me what Beauty is.

The Questioner. It seems to me quite simple. Beauty is—well—a thing is either beautiful, or it isn't. And—

The Artist. Just so; the only trouble is that so few of us are able to agree whether it is or isn't. You yourself have doubtless changed your opinions about what is beautiful many times in the course of your career as an art-lover; and the time may come when you will cherish some horrid nude of Matisse's as your dearest possession. Let us admit, like the wise old poet, that Beauty is not a thing which can be argued about. It can only be produced.

The Questioner. But if we don't know what Beauty is, how can we produce it?

The Artist. I have already told you—as the incidental result of creative effort.

The Questioner. Effort to create *what*?

The Artist. Oh, anything.

The Questioner. Are you joking?

The Artist. I never was more serious in my life. And I should really inform you that I am merely repeating the familiar commonplaces of modern esthetics. Beauty is the incidental result of the effort to create a house, a sword,—

The Questioner. Or a shoe?

The Artist. Yes. I have some peasant shoes from Russia which are very beautiful. You can see shoes which are works of art in any good museum.

The Questioner. But hardly in any boot-shop window!

The Artist. Those shoes were not created—they were done as a set task. They were not made by peasants or craftsmen for pleasure—they were made by wage-slaves who did them only because they must. Do not for a moment imagine that it is the difference in materials or shape that matters—it is the difference in the spirit with which they are made. I have seen modern shoes which are works of art—because they were made by a bootmaker who is an artist and does what pleases himself.

THE QUESTIONER. Do they please anybody else?

THE ARTIST. Eh?

THE QUESTIONER. Would you be seen wearing them?

THE ARTIST. Would I be seen drinking my coffee from a cup that had been turned on a wheel by a man who loved the feel of the clay under his fingers and who knew just the right touch to give the brim? Was Richard Coeur du Lion's sword less a sword because it had been made by an artist who dreamed over the steel instead of by a tired man in a hurry? I cannot afford to wear shoes made by my bootmaker-artist friend—but I wish I could, for they *fit*!

THE QUESTIONER. Will you give me his address?—I beg your pardon—Please go on.

THE ARTIST. I was about to say, you wrong the artist if you think that he is not interested in utility. It is only because utility has become bound up with slavery that artists and people with artistic impulses revolt against it and in defiance produce utterly and fantastically useless things. This will be so, as long as being useful means being a slave. But art is not an end in itself; it had its origin, and will find its destiny, in the production of useful things. For example—

THE QUESTIONER. Yes, do let us get down to the concrete!

THE ARTIST. Suppose you are out walking in a hilly country, and decide to whittle yourself a stick. Your wish is to make something useful. But you can't help making it more than useful. You can't help it, because, if you are not in a hurry, and nobody else is bossing the job, you find other impulses besides the utilitarian one coming in to elaborate your task. Shall I name those impulses?

THE QUESTIONER. If you will.

THE ARTIST. I am not a psychologist, but I would call them the impulse to command and the impulse to obey.

THE QUESTIONER. To command and obey *what*?

THE ARTIST. Your material, whatever it is—paint and canvas, words, sounds, clay, marble, iron. In this case, the stick of wood.

THE QUESTIONER. I'm afraid I do not quite—

THE ARTIST. The impulse to command comes first—the impulse to just show that stick who is master! the desire to impose your imperial will upon it. I suppose you might call it Vanity. And that impulse alone would result in your making something fantastic and grotesque or strikingly absurd—and yet beautiful in its way. But it is met and checked by the other impulse—the impulse to obey. No man that ever whittled wood but has felt that impulse. He feels that he must not do simply what he wants to do, but also what the wood *wants done* to it. The real artist does not care to treat marble as if it were soft, nor paint and canvas as though they were three-dimensional. He could if he wanted to—but he respects his medium. There is an instinctive pleasure in letting it have its way. I suppose you might call it Reverence. And this Vanity and this Reverence, the desire to command and the desire to obey, when they are set free in the dream and effort of creation, produce something which is more than useful. That *something more* is what we call Beauty.—Do you care to have me go further into the mechanics of beauty?

The Questioner. Well—er—I suppose now that we have got this far into the subject, we might as well get to the end of it. Go on!

The Artist. What I am about to tell you is the only really important thing about art. Unfortunately, the facts at issue have never been studied by first-class scientific minds, and so they lack a proper terminology to make them clear. In default of such a scientific terminology, we are forced to use the word "rhythm" in the special sense in which artists understand it. You speak of the movements of a dance as being rhythmic. The artist understands the word to refer to the relation of these movements to each other and above all to the emotion which they express. And to him the whole world is a dance, full of rhythmic gestures. The gesture of standing still, or of being asleep, is also rhythmic; the body is itself a gesture—he will speak of the rhythm of the line of a lifted arm or a bent knee. Trees that lift their branches to the sky, and rocks that sleep on the ground have their rhythms—every tree and every rock its own special rhythm. The rhythm of a pine tree is different from that of a palm—the rhythm of granitic rocks different from that of limestone. So far the matter is simple enough. But the relations of these rhythms to each other are also rhythmic. These relations are in fact so manifold that they constitute a chaos. But in this chaos each person feels a different rhythm; and, according as he has the power, transmits his sense of it to us through a rhythmic treatment of his medium. In the presence of his work, we feel what he has felt about the world; but we feel something more than that—we feel also the rhythm of the struggle in the artist between his impulse to command and his impulse to obey. Our own impulses of vanity and of reverence go out to welcome his power and his faithfulness. And just as there are gay rhythms and sad rhythms in the gesture of movement, so there are magnificent rhythms and trivial rhythms in the gesture of a soul facing the chaos of the world. What has he found worth while to play with, and how has he played with it? What kind of creator is he? Ability to feel and express significant rhythm—that is nine-tenths of art.

The Questioner. But my dear fellow, how are we to teach all this to children?

The Artist. Very simply: by giving them a knife and a piece of wood.

The Questioner. Well, really!

The Artist. And crayons and clay and singing-games and so forth.—But perhaps you prefer to show them pictures of alleged masterpieces, and tell them, "This is great art!" They will believe you, of course; and they will hate great art ever afterwards—just as they hate great poetry, and for the same excellent reason: because, presented to them in that way, it is nothing but a damned nuisance. Yet the child who enjoys hearing and telling a story has in him the capacity to appreciate and perhaps to create the greatest of stories; and the child who enjoys whittling a block of wood has in him the capacity to appreciate and perhaps to create the greatest art!

THE QUESTIONER. Then you do not think children can be taught to appreciate art by looking at photographic reproductions of it?

THE ARTIST. I would hardly expect a Fiji Islander to become an appreciator of civilized music by letting him look at my phonograph records. The dingy-brownish photograph of a gloriously colored painting has even less educational value—for it lies about the original. Do you know that there are thousands and thousands of American school children who think that the great masterpieces of the world's painting are the color of axle-grease? They are never told that their own free efforts with colored crayons are more like Botticelli in every sense than any photograph could possibly be; but it is true.

THE QUESTIONER. But don't you want them to *respect* Botticelli?

THE ARTIST. No. I want them to look at Botticelli's pictures as they look at those of another child—free to criticize, free to dislike, free to scorn. For only when you are free to despise, are you free to admire. After all, who was Botticelli? Another child. Perhaps they may prefer Goya—

THE QUESTIONER. Or the Sunday comic supplement!

THE ARTIST. A healthy taste. And if they know what drawing is, though having used a pencil themselves, they will prefer the better comic pictures to the worse, and be ready to appreciate Goya and Daumier—who were the super-Sunday-supplement comic artists of their day.

THE QUESTIONER. Left to themselves they may come to like Goya, as you say; but will they ever come to appreciate such a masterpiece as Leonardo's Last Supper without some more formal teaching?

THE ARTIST. Do you call it "teaching" to talk solemnly to children in language they cannot understand? If they are making pictures themselves, and being assisted in their enthusiastic experiments by a real artist instead of a teacher, they will naturally wonder why their friend should have the photograph of the Last Supper in the portfolio from which he is always taking out some picture in order to illustrate his answers to their questions. And having wondered, they will ask why, and their friend will tell them; and perhaps they will get some of their friends enthusiasm, and perhaps not. But they will know that the real human being who is like themselves *does* like that picture.

THE QUESTIONER. But it makes no difference whether *they* like it or not?

THE ARTIST. You can't compel them to like it, can you? You can only compel them to pretend that they do.

THE QUESTIONER. Can't you teach them what is called "good taste"?

THE ARTIST. Only too easily. And their "good taste" will lead them infallibly to prefer the imitations of what they have been taught to praise, and quite as infallibly to reject the great new art of their generation. They will think some new Whistler a pot of paint flung in the public's face, and the next Cezanne a dauber.

THE QUESTIONER. Then you don't approve of good taste!

THE ARTIST. Every artist despises it, and the people who have it. We know quite well that the people who pretend to like Titian and Turner, because they have been carefully taught that it is the thing to do, would have turned up their noses at Titian and Turner in their own day—because they were not on the list of dead artists whom it was the fashion to call great; they know moreover that these same people of good taste are generally incapable of distinguishing between a beautiful and an ugly wall-paper, between a beautiful and an ugly plate, or even between a beautiful and an ugly necktie! Outside the bounds of their memorized list, they have no taste whatever.

THE QUESTIONER. Cannot good taste be taught so as to include the whole of life?

THE ARTIST. It would take too much time. And thank God for that! For good taste is simply a polite pretense by which we cover up our lack of that real sense of beauty which comes only from intimate acquaintance with creative processes. The most cultivated people in the world cannot produce beauty by merely having notions about it. But the most uncultivated people in the world cannot help producing beauty if only they have time to dream as they work—if only they have freedom to let their work become something besides utilitarian.

THE QUESTIONER. You think, then, that education should not concern itself with good taste, but rather with creative effort?

THE ARTIST. Exactly.

THE QUESTIONER. You say that children are artists already?

THE ARTIST. And that artists are children.

THE QUESTIONER. Then the task of education in respect to them would seem to be easy!

THE ARTIST. No—on the contrary, infinitely hard!

THE QUESTIONER. What do you mean?

The Artist. I have said that children are artists and that artists are children. The task of education is to help them to *grow up*.

THE QUESTIONER. New difficulties!

THE ARTIST. And tremendous ones! But if I am to discuss them, you must keep still for a while and let me talk in my own fashion.

—Very well, ladies and gentlemen. Shall we adjourn for lunch, and when we reassemble here give the Artist the platform for half an hour? What is the sentiment of the meeting? The Ayes have it.

XVII.

The Artist as a Child.

WITHOUT any further delay, the Artist shall now address you.—Please take the platform, sir!

"My friends! We are gathered here today to consider how to implant in the youthful and innocent minds which are entrusted to our care the beneficent and holy influences of that transcendent miracle which we know as Art. Sacred and mysterious subject that it is, we approach it with bated—"

Wait! wait! There is some mistake here, I am sure. Just a moment!—

"We approach with bated breath these austere and sacred—"

Stop, I say!

"Austere and sacred regions—"

Usher, will you please throw this fellow out! He is not the man we were listening to this morning—he is a rank impostor, who has disguised himself as an artist in order to befuddle our deliberations with mystagogical cant. If you will pull off that false beard, I think you will find that he is a well-known Chautauqua lecturer. . . . Aha, I thought so!—Shame on you! And now get out of here as quickly as you can!—Ah, there comes the real Artist—late, as usual. What have you to say for yourself?

"I'm sorry—I got to thinking of something else, and nearly forgot to come back here. Which brings me at once to the heart of what I want to say. Artists, as I have said, are children—and, children that they are, they forget the errands upon which the world sends them. They forget, because these errands are not part of their own life. You reproach us with being careless and irresponsible—but if you will study the child at play or the artist at work, you will discover that he is not careless or irresponsible in regard to his own concerns. But this deep divorce between the concerns of the artist and the child and the concerns of the world is the tragic problem for which we now seek a solution. The world has been unable to solve it. It has only made the breach deeper.

"For the world does not know that its work can be play, that adult life can be a game like the games of children, only with more desperate and magnificent issues. It does not reflect that we gather sticks in the wood with infinite happy patience and labour to build our bonfires because those bonfires are our own dream creatively realized; and it cannot think of any better way to get us to bring in the wood for the kitchen stove than to say, 'Johnny, I've told you three times to bring in that wood, and if you can't mind I'll have your father interview you in the woodshed.' In brief, it presents our participation in adult life as meaningless toil performed at the bidding of another under coercion. And the whole of adult life gradually takes on this same aspect. We are to do the bidding of another in office or factory because otherwise we will starve.

"So the child-artist unwillingly becomes a slave. But there are some children who rebel against slavery. They prefer to keep their dreams. They are regarded with disapproval and anxiety by their families, who tell them that they must grow up. But they do not want to grow up into slavery. They want to remain free. They want to make their dreams come true.

"'But who will pay for your dreams?' the world asks. And it is not pleasant to face the possibility of starving to death. And so they comfort themselves with the illusion of fame and wealth. Sometimes their families are cajoled into investing in this rather doubtful speculative enterprise, and the child-artist becomes an artist-child, supported through life by his parents, and playing busily at his art. Sometimes the speculation turns out well financially, the illusion of success becomes a reality; but this, however gratifying to the artist as a justification of his career, is not his own reason for being an artist. The 'successful' artist has a child-like pleasure in the awe of really grown-up people at the material proofs of his importance; and if he has given hostages to fortune, if he must support a family of his own, he may ploddingly reproduce the happy accidents of his creative effort which gained him these rewards; but he feels that in so doing he has ceased to be a free man and become a slave—and all too often, as we know from the shocked comment of the world, he renounces these rewards, becomes a child at play again, and lets his wife and children get along as best they may. He yearns, perhaps, for fame—as a sort of public consent to his going on being a child. But whether he starves in the garret or bows from his limousine to admiring crowds, what he really wants of the world is just permission to play. He is not interested in the affairs of the world.

"There are exceptions, of course. There are poets and musicians and painters who take an interest in the destinies of mankind; but this is regarded by their fellow-artists as a kind of heresy or disloyalty—much as school children (or college boys) regard the behaviour of one who really takes his school work seriously. The public also is accustomed to regard the artist as a child; they laugh at his 'ideas' about practical affairs—though often enough they adopt his ideas in dead earnest later. Shelley, for instance, proposed to conduct campaigns of education by dropping leaflets from balloons. 'A quaint idea, characteristic of his visionary and impractical mind,' said his biographers; and then, having laughed at the idea, the world in its Great War proceeds to adopt that idea and carry it out on a tremendous scale. . . .

"When the child refuses to be a slave, he is thenceforth excluded by common consent from the affairs of the grown-up world. And as the breach widens between the artist and the world, as the world becomes more and more committed to slavery, the artist is more consciously and wilfully a child. He is forbidden by the growing public opinion of his group to write or sing about human destinies. 'The artist must not be a propagandist,' it is declared indignantly. And finally it comes to such a pass that it is not artistic good-form for the artist to tell stories which the public can understand—the painter is prohibited from making images which the common man is able to recognize—the musician scorns to compose tunes which anybody could dance to or whistle! And all this is simply the child's defiance to the world—his games are his own, and the grown-ups can keep their hands off! If adult life is slavery (which it is), he will be damned before he will have anything to do with it.

"And he is damned—damned to a childishness which contains only the stubborn wilfulness of the child's playing, but has forgotten its motive. That motive is different from his. He has changed from the child who played at being a man, to a man who plays at being a child. The child's dreams were large, and his are small. The child took all life for his province—was by turns a warrior, a blacksmith, a circus-rider, a husband, a store-keeper, a fireman, a savage, an undertaker. The child-artist wanted to play at everything. The artist-child has renounced these magnificent ambitions. The world may conscript him to fight in its wars, but he refuses to bother his head as to what they are about; if he finds that he has to walk up-town because there is a street-car strike, he is mildly annoyed, but (I am describing an extreme but not infrequent type) he declines to interest himself in the labour movement; he escapes from the responsibilities of a serious love-affair on the ground that 'an artist should never marry'; he pays his grocery bills, or leaves them unpaid, but the co-operative movement bores him; and so on! He is content to live in that little corner of life in which he can play undisturbed by worldly interests. This type, I have said, is not infrequent; its perfect exemplars, the artists who were so completely children that they did not even know of the existence of the outside world, are revered as the saints of art, and often as its martyrs, which in truth they were; and they are admired by thousands of young artists who only aspire to such perfection, while shamefacedly admitting that they themselves are tainted with ordinary human interests.

"This is what the world has done to us; it has made us choose between being children in a tiny sphere all our lives, or going into the larger world of reality as slaves. And I think we have made the right choice. For we have kept alive in our childish folly the flame of a sacred revolt against slavery. We have succeeded in making the world envious of our freedom. We have shown it the only way to be happy.

"But the artist cannot get along without the world. His art springs from the commonest impulses of the human race, and those impulses are utilitarian at root; the savage who scratched the aurochs on the wall of his cave was hungry for meat and desirous of luck in the hunting tomorrow; the primitive Greeks who danced their seasonal dances from which sprang the glory of dramatic art, wanted the crops to grow; and that which we call great art everywhere is great only because it springs from a communal hunger and fulfils a communal wish. When art becomes divorced from the aspirations of the common man, all its technical perfection will not keep it alive; it revolts against its own technical perfection, and goes off into quaint and austere quests for new truths upon which to nourish itself; and only when it discovers the common man and fulfils his unfulfilled desires, does it flourish again. Art must concern itself with the world, or perish.

"Nor can the world get along without the artist. Slavery cannot keep it going—it needs the free impulses of the creative spirit. It needs the artist, not as a being to scorn and worship by turns, but as the worker-director of its activities. It needs the artist as blacksmith, husband, and store-keeper—as teacher, priest, and statesman. Only so can it endure and fulfil its destinies.

"But if the artist is to be all these things, if he is to enter into the activities of the real world instead of running away from them, he must grow up. And that is the task of education: to make a man of him without killing the artist. We must begin, then, before the artist in him is killed; we must begin with the child. So far as I can see, the school as it exists at present is utterly and hopelessly inadequate to the task. It requires a special mechanism, which happily exists in the outside world, and need only be incorporated into the educational system, in order to provide a medium of transition between the dream-creations of childhood and the realistic creativity of adult life. This mechanism is the Theatre."

XVIII.

The Drama of Education.

"BUT why—in the name of all that is beautiful!—*why* the Theatre?"

Ah! Who uttered that agonized cry of protest?

He comes forward.

"It was I who spoke. Do not, I beg of you, as you love Beauty, have any truck with the Theatre. Leave it alone—avoid it—flee it as you would the pestilence! I know what I am talking about!"

And who, pray, are you?

"I am an Actor!"

Well, well!—this is rather curious.

"Not at all! Who should know better than the Actor the dreadful truth about the Theatre—that it is the home of a base triviality, the citadel of insincerity, the last refuge of everything that is banal in thought and action!"

Really, the Theatre seems to have no friends nowadays except the professors who teach play-writing in the colleges! But I think we should hear what our friend the Artist has to say in its defence.

The Artist. "There is nothing wrong with the Theatre except what is wrong with the whole of modern life. Our newspapers are base and trivial, our politics are insincere, and the products of our slave-system of production have a banality which Broadway could scarcely surpass. In all these fields of effort, as in the Theatre, the creative spirit has surrendered to the slave-system. But in the Theatre, and in no place else in the world, we find the modes of child-life, of primitive creative activity, surviving intact into adult life. What is costume but the 'dressing-up' of childhood, the program with its cast of characters but a way of saying 'Let's pretend!'—what, in short, is the Playhouse but a house of Play? It is all there—the singing and dancing, the make-believe, the whole paraphernalia of child creativity: it is true that the game is played by children who are not free to create their own dreams, who must play always at some one else's bidding, half children and half slaves! But—and this is its importance to us—the Theatre is the place where the interests of the child meet and merge into those of the adult. It is the natural transition between dreams and realities. And it is thereby the bridge across the gulf that separates art from the world.

"Let me explain. When I use the phrase 'The Theatre,' I am not thinking of the dramatic arts in any restricted and special sense. For the Theatre, as the original source of all the arts, the spring from which half a hundred streams have poured, into the separate arts of music, dancing, singing, poetry, pageantry, and what not—the Theatre in its historic aspect as the spirit of communal festivity—is significant to us not as the vehicle of a so-called dramatic art, separate and distinct from the arts which go to make it up, but rather as the institution which preserves the memory of the common origin of all these arts and which still has the power to unite them in the service of a common purpose. In the Theatre, as in the child's playing, they are not things alien from each other and isolate from life, but parts of each other and of a greater thing—the expressing of a common emotion.

"So when I speak of making the Theatre a part of the educational system in the interest of art and artists, I mean to suggest a union of all the arts in the expression of communal purposes and emotions through a psychological device of which the Theatre, even in its contemporary form, stands as a ready-to-hand example.

"I cannot be sufficiently grateful to the Theatre for continuing to exist, in however trivial or base a form. Suppose it had perished for ever from the earth! Who would be so daring a theorist as to conceive the project of bringing together the story-teller, the poet, the musician, the singer, the dancer, the pantomimist, the painter, in the co-operative enterprise of creating 'one common wave of thought and joy lifting mankind again'? Who, if such a thing were proposed, would have any idea what was being talked about? As it is, however, I can point to any musical comedy on Broadway and say, 'What I mean is something like that, only quite different!'

"Different, because the communal emotions which these artists would have joined themselves together to express would hardly be, if they were left free to decide the question themselves, the mere emotions of mob-anxiety, mob-lasciviousness and mob-humour which are the three motifs of commercial drama. No, you have to pay people to get them to take part in that dull and tawdry game! When they do things to suit themselves, as they sometimes adventurously do even now, it is something that it is more fun to play at. As free men and women they cannot help being artists, they must needs choose that their play shall be a 'work of art whose rhythms fulfil some deep wish of the human soul.—'"

"Just a moment! Some one, I think, wants to ask a question.—Louder, please!"

"I said—this is all very well as a plea for a Free Theatre, but what has it to do with Education?"

The Artist. "Evidently I have not made myself clear. The problem of Education with respect to Art is to keep alive the child's creative impulses, and use them in the real world of adult life. We don't want to kill the artist in him; nor do we want to keep him a child all his life in some tiny corner of the world, apart from its serious activities. We don't want the slave who has forgotten how to play, nor the dreamer who is afraid of realities. We want an education which will merge the child's play into the man's life, the artist's dreams into the citizen's labours. The Theatre—"

"Excuse me, but what I can't see is how a Children's Theatre is going to do all that! Even if you put a theatre in every school-building—"

THE ARTIST. "You quite mistake my meaning. I would rather confiscate the theatres and put a school into each of them; and so, for that matter, would I do with the factories! But, unfortunately, I am not Minister of Public Education. In default of that, what I propose is small enough—but it is not so small as you suppose when you think that I want to set children to rehearsing plays and making scenery for a school play. I propose rather that the spirit of the Theatre—the spirit of creative play—should enter into every branch of the school work, until the school itself becomes a Theatre—a gorgeous, joyous, dramatic festival of learning-to-live.

"Think how real History would become if it were dramatized by the children themselves! I do not mean its merely picturesque moments, but its real meanings, acted out—the whole drama of human progress—a group of cave-men talking of the days before men knew how to make fire—Chaldean traders, Babylonian princes, Egyptian slaves, each with his story to tell—Greek citizens discussing politics just before the election—a wounded London artisan hiding from the King's soldiers in a garret, and telling his shelterer the true story of Wat Tyler's rebellion—a French peasant just before the Revolution, and his son who has been reading a strange book by that man Rousseau in which it is declared that there is no such thing as the Divine Right of Kings. . . .

"Mathematics as an organized creative effort centering around real planning and building and measuring and calculating. . . .

"Geography—a magnificent voyaging in play all round the world and in reality all round the town and surrounding countryside. . . . A scientific investigation of the natural resources of the community, its manufactures, exports and imports, discussed round bonfires in the woods by the committee at the end of a long day's tramp, and the final drawing up of their report, to be illustrated on the screen by photographs taken by themselves. . . . The adventure of map-making. . . .

"(You get the idea, don't you? You see *why* it is more real than ordinary education—*because* it is all play!)

"And all these delightful games brought together in grand pageants—instead of examinations!—every half year. . . .

"That is what I mean.

"Making whatever teaching of art there may be, part and parcel with these activities—and using the school-theatre, if one exists, *not* to produce Sheridan's 'Rivals' in, but as a convenience to the presentation of the drama of their own education; but in any case making all their world a stage, not forgetting that first and best stage of all, God's green outdoors!

"No, I say, I do not want to put a theatre into every school—I want every school to be a Theatre in which a Guild of Young Artists will learn to do the work of the world without ceasing to be free and happy.

"I hope I have succeeded in making myself clear?"

XIX.
The Drama of Life.

AS to his immediate proposals, I think the Artist has made himself quite clear. But he opened up an interesting vista of possibilities when he spoke of being Minister of Public Education. He said he couldn't do certain things because he wasn't Minister of Public Education. What we would like very much to know is what he would do if he were!—Do you mind telling us?

The Artist. "In the first place I would set fire to—But you are sure I am not taking up your time unduly?"

No, no! Go on!

The Artist. "I would set fire to the coat-tails of all the present boards of education who are now running our educational system in complete indifference to the interests of the child. I would institute democratic control: turn the school system over to the National Guild of Young Artists. My career as an educational autocrat would necessarily stop right there, so far as the internal revolutionizing of education is concerned—for what I have been telling you is simply what I think the children themselves would do with the schools if they were allowed to run them.

"But Education, as I understand it, does not stop short with the school—it extends throughout all life. It is what I would call the civilizing process. And there is much to be done to many departments of life before they can become part of a real civilizing process. I will describe only one, but not the least fundamental of these changes—the democratizing of the Theatre. Or rather, as I should say, turning it into a school.

"A school of what? you will ask. A school of life, of aspiration, of progress, of civilization. It can be all these things if it becomes the People's Theatre. Therefore, as Minister of Public Education, I propose to confiscate the Theatres and turn them over to the People.

"But again, when I speak of 'The Theatre,' I do not mean merely the buildings in which plays are given. I mean all those arts which are part of communal creativity. I propose to unite them all in communal festivals of human progress. I do not propose that we shall begin by holding classes in the Hippodrome—though that will come. I propose to begin with solemn and magnificent national holiday pageants similar to those which were so frequently and gorgeously celebrated during the days of the great French Revolution—"

At this moment a policeman approaches the stage.

"I wish to warn the speaker that everything he says is being taken down in shorthand by one of our men, and if he wants to finish his speech the less he says about Revolution the better. That's all."

The Artist. "Thank you! I should have said, during the days of a certain great political and social upheaval which laid the foundations of modern life in general, and of our gallant ally, the French Republic, in particular. The historic festivals of which I speak were in charge of the great artists and composers of the nation, and their art and music were used to express the common emotion and purpose of the People. So it will be with ours. Our artists will unite to express the new ideals of mankind, and together with each other and with the People, will lay the foundations of a new and democratic art.

"It is here that the theatres, which will already be in charge of the guilds of artists, will come into play. For the new art must have a solid basis in popular emotions such as only the theatre can give. They will therefore present plays which criticize the old slave-system, satirize its manners, its traditional heroes, its ideals; plays which invest with tragic dignity the age-long struggle of the People against oppressive institutions and customs; plays which creatively foreshadow a new popular culture and morality; and plays which celebrate the final victory of the People in their revolutionary strug—"

Another policeman:

"Are ye making an address on education, or trying to incite to riot? L'ave that word Revolution alone.—This is the second time we're warning ye."

The Artist. "I'm sorry. I had hoped to show the influence of the national aspirations of a great Celtic people upon their artistic life, and the final flowering of their dreams in a certain political and social upheaval—"

The Policeman. "Oh, ye mean the Irish Revolution? That's different! Ye're all right. Go on!"

The Artist. "My time, however, is short. I shall leave to your imagination the means to be used in furthering these aims by the democratization of technical artistic culture. I shall speak only of its spiritual aspects. The Theatre, as I have said, will take the lead in preparing for the new day by presenting plays which will teach the People courage and confidence in their destiny, teach them to scorn the ideals of the traditional past, deepen their sense of community with the People in all lands in their world-wide struggle for freedom, and make them face the future with a clear and unshakable resolution, an indomitable will to victory.

"If I had time, I should like to tell you how this educational program is already being carried out, in spite of the greatest difficulties, by a certain Slavic nation—"

Another interruption!—by a red-faced, dictatorial, imperatorial personage who has been sitting there all this time, swelling with rage and awaiting his opportunity. He speaks:

"Officer! I am a member of the Board of Education, and I demand that you arrest that man as a Bolshevik agitator!"

(Tumultuous scenes.)

XX.

Curiosity.

LET us, my friends, pass over this unfortunate incident, and get on to the next thing as quickly as possible. The next thing on our program is Truth. The one who best understands Truth is undoubtedly the Philosopher.—Here he is, and we shall commence without delay. Will some one volunteer to conduct the examination? Thank you, madam. Go right ahead.

The Lady. We wish to ask you a few questions.

The Philosopher. Certainly, madam. What about?

The Lady. About Truth.

The Philosopher. Dear, dear!

The Lady. Whom are you addressing?

The Philosopher. I beg your pardon!—It was only an exclamation of surprise. It has been so long since anybody has talked to me about Truth. How quaint and refreshing!

The Lady. Please do not be frivolous.

The Philosopher. I am sorry—but really, it *is* amusing. Tell me, to which school do you belong?

The Lady. To the Julia Richmond High School, if you must know—though I don't see what that has to do with Truth.

The Philosopher. Oh! You mean you are a school-teacher!

The Lady. Certainly. Doesn't that suit you?

The Philosopher. It delights me. I feared at first you might be a Hegelian, or even a Platonist. Now that I find you are a Pragmatist like myself—

The Lady. Pragmatist? Yes, I have heard of Pragmatism. William James—summer course in Philosophy. But why do you think I am a Pragmatist?

The Philosopher. A school-teacher *must* be a pragmatist, madam, or go mad. If you really believed the human brain to be an instrument capable of accurate thinking, your experiences with your pupils and your principal, not to speak of your boards of education, would furnish you a spectacle of human wickedness and folly too horrible to be endured. But you realize that the poor things were never intended to think.

The Lady. That's true; they're doing the best they can, aren't they? They just *can't* believe anything they don't want to believe!

The Philosopher. That is to say, man is not primarily a thinking animal—he is a creature of emotion and action.

The Lady. Especially action. They are always in such a hurry to get something done that they really can't stop to think about it! But I'm afraid all this is really beside the point. What we want to know is why the school fails so miserably in its attempt to teach children to think?

The Philosopher. Perhaps it is in too much of a hurry. But are you sure you really want children to learn to think?

The Lady. Of course we do!

The Philosopher. The greatest part of life, you know, can be lived without thought. We do not think about where we put our feet as we walk along an accustomed road. We leave that to habit. We do not think about how to eat, once we have learned to do it in a mannerly way. The accountant does not think about how to add a column of figures—he has his mind trained to the task. And there is little that cannot be done by the formation of proper habits, to the complete elimination of thought. The habits will even take care of the regulation of the emotions. For all practical purposes, don't you agree with me that thinking might be dispensed with?

The Lady. I hardly know whether to take you seriously or not—

The Philosopher. Can you deny what I say?

The Lady. But—but life isn't all habit. We must think—in order to make—decisions.

The Philosopher. It is not customary. We let our wishes fight it out, and the strongest has its way. But I once knew a man who did think in order to make his decisions. The result was that he always made them too late. And what was worse, the habit grew upon him. He got to thinking about everything he wanted to do, with the result that he couldn't do anything. I told him that he'd have to stop thinking—that it wasn't healthy. Finally he went to a doctor, and sure enough the doctor told him that it was a well known disease—a neurosis. Its distinguishing mark was that the patient always saw two courses open to him everywhere he turned—two alternatives, two different ways of doing something, two women between whom he must choose, two different theories of life, and so on to distraction. The reason for it, the doctor said, was that the patient's will, that is to say the functioning of his emotional wish-apparatus, had become deranged, and the burden of decision was being put upon a part of the mind incapable of bearing it—the logical faculty. He cured my friend's neurosis, and now he thinks no more about the practical affairs of life than you or I or anybody else. So you see thinking is abnormal—even dangerous. Why do you want to teach children to think?

The Lady. Well—it is rather taken for granted that the object of education is learning to think.

The Philosopher. But is that true? If it is, why do you teach your children the multiplication table, or the rule that the square of the hypotenuse of a right triangle is equal to the sum of the squares of the other two sides—unless in order to save them the trouble of thinking? By the way, what is the capital of Tennessee, and when did Columbus discover America?

The Lady. Nashville, 1492. Why?

The Philosopher You didn't have to stop to think, did you? Your memory has been well trained. But if you will forgive the comparison, so has my dog's been well trained; when I say, 'Towser, show the lady your tricks,' he goes through an elaborate performance that would gladden your heart, for he is an apt pupil; but I don't for a moment imagine that I have taught him to think.

The Lady. Then you don't want children taught the multiplication table?

The Philosopher. I? Most certainly I do. And so far as I am concerned, I would gladly see a great many other short cuts in mathematics taught, so as to save our weary human brains the trouble of thinking about such things. I am in fact one of the Honorary Vice-Presidents of the Society for the Elimination of Useless Thinking.

The Lady. I am afraid you are indulging in a jest.

The Philosopher. I am afraid I am. But if you knew Philosophers better you would realize that it is a habit of ours to jest about serious matters. It is one of our short-cuts to wisdom. Read your Plato and William James again. Delightful humorists, both of them, I assure you. I fear you went to them too soberly, and in too much of a hurry.

The Lady. Doubtless your jokes have a historic sanctity, since you say so, but I do not feel that they have advanced our inquiry very much.

The Philosopher. I abhor myself and repent in dust and ashes. What do you want to know?

The Lady. I want to know what is the use of thinking?

The Philosopher. Ah, my jest was not in vain, if it provoked you to that. I should call that question the evidence of a real thought.

The Lady. Well, what is the answer?

The Philosopher. Oh, please don't stop, now that you have made such a good start! Think again, and answer your own question.

The Lady. Hm. . . .

The Philosopher. Yes?

The Lady. I was thinking of Newton and the apple. If it hadn't been for Newton's ability to think, he would never have formulated the law of gravitation.

The Philosopher. And what a pity that would have been—wouldn't it?

The Lady. You mean that it makes very little practical difference to us?

The Philosopher. It would if the town were being bombarded. The Newtonian calculations are considered useful by the artillery schools. But it is true that it was Newton and not an artillery officer who made them.

The Lady. You mean that the artillery captain would have been too intent on practical matters?

The Philosopher. And in too much of a hurry. Then there's the steam-engine. Useful invention—the very soul of hurry. Who invented it—some anxious postilion who thought horses were too slow? Or somebody whose mind was so empty of practical concerns that it could be intrigued by a tea-kettle? And by the way, it was Stephenson, wasn't it, who applied the steam-principle to locomotion? I've a very poor memory, but I think Watt's engine was just a toy. No practical use whatever. Other people found out the practical uses for it. Arkwright. Fulton. Hoe. Et cetera.

The Lady. I see. The results of thinking may be put to use afterward, but the motive for thinking is not the desire to produce such results. I wonder if that is true?

The Philosopher. What is the common reproach against philosophers and scientists?

The Lady. That they are impractical. But inventors—

The Philosopher. Did you ever know an inventor?

The Lady. Yes. . . .

The Philosopher. Was he rich?

The Lady. He starved to death.

The Philosopher. Why?

The Lady. Because every one said that his invention was very wonderful, but not of the slightest use to anybody. . . . Yes, it's true.

The Philosopher. That the results of thinking do not provide the motive for thinking?

The Lady. Yes.

The Philosopher. Then what is the motive for thinking?

The Lady. Just—curiosity, I suppose!

The Philosopher. Disinterested curiosity?

The Lady. Yes.

The Philosopher. Then in the interests of scientific truth we should cultivate disinterested curiosity?

The Lady. Doubtless.

The Philosopher. How would you go about doing so?

The Lady. I don't know.

The Philosopher. By hurriedly thrusting upon the minds of the children in your charge so great a multitude of interests as to leave them no time to wonder about anything?

The Lady. That would hardly seem to be the way to do it. But—

The Philosopher. When Newton looked at his famous apple, was there anyone there who said, "Now, Newton, look at this apple. Look at this apple, I say! Consider the apple. First, it is round. Second, it is red. Third, it is sweet. This is the Truth about apples. Now let me see if you have grasped what I have told you. What are the three leading facts about apples? What! Don't you remember? Shame on you! I fear I will have to report you to the mayor!"—did anything like that happen?

The Lady. Newton was not a child.

The Philosopher. You should have talked to Newton's family about him. That is just what they said he was! I will admit that if you left children free to wonder about things instead of forcing the traditional aspects of those things upon their attention, they might not all become great scientists. But are you a great archaeologist?

The Lady. No!

The Philosopher. Did you ever go on a personally conducted tour of the ruins of Rome, and have the things you were to see and think pointed out to you by a guide?

The Lady. Yes, and I hated it!

The Philosopher. You are not a great archaeologist and you never expect to be one, and yet you thought you could get more out of those ruins yourself than with the assistance of that pesky guide. You preferred to be free—to see or not to see, to wonder and ponder and look again or pass by. And don't you think the children in your charge might enjoy their trip a little more if they didn't have to listen to the mechanically unctuous clatter of a guide?

The Lady. If one could only be sure they wouldn't just waste their time!

The Philosopher. Madam, are you quite sure that you, as a teacher, are not wasting *your* time?

The Lady. You make me wonder whether that may not be possible. But sheer idleness—

The Philosopher. Was Newton busy when he lay down under that tree? Did he have an appointment with the apple? Did he say he would give it ten minutes, and come again next day if it seemed worth while? What is disinterested curiosity, in plain English?

The Lady. Idle curiosity—I fear.

The Philosopher. I fear you are right. Then you would say that the way to approach Truth, in school and out, is to cultivate idle curiosity?

The Lady. I did not intend to say anything of the kind. But you compel me to say it.

The Philosopher. I compel you? Deny it if you wish!

The Lady. I thought you were going to answer my questions, and you have been making me answer yours!

The Philosopher. That is also an ancient habit of our profession. But since you have now arrived, of your own free will, at an inescapable if uncomfortable conclusion, you can now have no further need for my services, and I bid you all good day!

XXI.

The Right to be Wrong.

ONE moment!—I take it, my friends, we are agreed in demanding of the Philosopher that he condescend to some concrete and practical suggestions in regard to education.—Briefly, please!

The Philosopher. "You must draw your own conclusions. Traditional education is based on the assumption that knowledge is a mass of information which can be given to the child in little dabs at regular intervals. We know, however, that the education based on this assumption is a failure. It kills rather than stimulates curiosity; and without curiosity, information is useless. We are thus forced to realize that knowledge does not reside outside the child, but in the contact of the child with the world through the medium of curiosity. And thus the whole emphasis of education is changed. We no longer seek to educate the child—we only attempt to give him the opportunity to educate himself. He alone has the formula of his own specific needs; none of us is wise enough to arrange for him the mysterious series of beautiful and poignant contacts with reality by which alone he can 'learn.' This means that he must choose his own lessons. And if you think that, left to choose, he would prefer no lessons at all, you are quite mistaken. Let me remind you that children are notoriously curious about everything—everything except, as you will very justly point out, the things people want them to know. It then remains for us to refrain from forcing any kind of knowledge upon them, and they will be curious about everything. You may imagine that they will prefer only the less complex kinds of knowledge; but do you regard children's games as simple? They are in fact exceedingly complex. And they are all the more interesting because they are complex. We ourselves with our adult minds, penetrate cheerfully into the complexities of baseball, or embroidery, or the stock-market, following the lead of some natural curiosity; and if our minds less often penetrate into the complexities of music, or science, it is because these things have associations which bring them within the realm of the dutiful. Evolutionary biology is far more interesting than stamp-collecting; but it is, unfortunately, made to seem not so delightfully useless, and hence it is shunned by adolescent boys and girls. But postage-stamp collecting can be made as much a bore as biology; it needs only to be put into the schools as a formal course.

"Consider for a moment the boy stamp-collector. His interest in his collection is in the nature of a passion. Does it astonish you that passionateness should be the fruit of idle curiosity? Then you need to face the facts of human psychology. The boy's passion for his collection of stamps is akin to the passion of the scientist and the poet. Do you desire of children that they should have a similar passion for arithmetic, for geography, for history? Then you must leave them free to find out the interestingness of these things. There is no way to passionate interest save through the gate of curiosity; and curiosity is born of idleness. But doubtless you have a quite wrong notion of what idleness means. Idleness is not doing nothing. Idleness is *being free to do anything*. To be forced to do nothing is not idleness, it is the worst kind of imprisonment. Being made to stand in the corner with one's face to the wall is not idleness—it is punishment. But getting up on Saturday morning with a wonderful day ahead in which one may do what one likes—that is idleness. And it leads straight into tremendous expenditures of energy. There is a saying, 'The devil finds some mischief still for idle hands to do.' Yes, but why should the devil have no competition? And that, as I understand it, is the function of education—to provide for idle and happy children fascinating contacts with reality—through games, tools, books, scientific instruments, gardens, and older persons with passionate interests in science and art and handicraft.

"Such a place would in a few respects resemble the schools we know; but the spirit would be utterly different from the spirit of traditional education. The apparatus for arousing the child's curiosity would be infinitely greater than the meagre appliances of our public schools; but however great, the child would be the centre of it all—not as the object of a process, but as the possessor of the emotions by force of which all these outward things become Education.

"But, you may ask, what has all this to do with truth? Simply this. We have been forcing children to memorize alleged facts. A fact so memorized cannot be distinguished from a falsehood similarly memorized. And so we may very well say that we have failed to bring truth into education. For truth is reality brought into vital contact with the mind. It makes no difference whether we teach children that the earth is round or flat, if it means nothing to them either way. For truth does not reside in something outside the child's mind; reality becomes truth only when it is made a part of his living.

"But, you will protest—and you will protest the more loudly the more you know of children—that their processes of thought are illogical, fantastic and wayward. And you will ask, Do I mean that we must respect the child's error in order to cultivate in him a love of truth? Yes, I do mean just that! Do I mean that we must respect the child's belief that the earth is flat, you ask? More than that, we must respect a thousand obscure and pervasive childish notions, such as the notion that a hair from a horse's tail will turn into a pollywog if left in the rainbarrel, or the notion that the way to find a lost ball is to spit on the back of the hand, repeat an incantation couched in such words as 'Spit, Spit, tell me where the ball is!' and then strike it with the palm of the other hand. You can doubtless supply a thousand instances of the kind of childhood thinking to which I refer. But for simplicity's sake, let us use the childish notion that the earth is flat as a convenient symbol for them all. And I say that if we do not respect the error, we shall not have any real success in convincing the child of the truth. We shall easily persuade him that the globe in the schoolroom is round—that the picture of the earth in the geography-book is round—but not that the familiar earth upon which he walks is anything but flat! At best, we shall teach him a secondary, literary, schoolroom conception to put beside his workaday one. And, in the long run, we shall place a scientific conception of things in general beside his primitive childish superstitions—but we shall scarcely displace them; and when it comes to a show-down in his adult life, we shall find him acting in accordance with childish superstitions rather than with scientific knowledge. Most of us, as adults, are full of such superstitions, and we act accordingly, and live feebly and fearfully; for we have never yielded to the childish magical conception of the world the respect that is due to it as a worthy opponent of scientific truth—we have assumed that we were persuaded of truth, while in reality truth has never yet met error in fair fight in our minds.

"If you wish to convince a friend of something, do you not first seek to find out what he really thinks about it, and make him weigh your truth and his error in the same balance? But in dealing with children, we fail to take account of their opinions at all. We say, 'You must believe this because it is so.' If they do believe it, they have only added one more superstition to their collection. Truths are *not* true because somebody says so; nor even because everybody says so; they are true only because they fit in better with all the rest of life than what we call errors—because they bear the test of living—because they work out. And this way of discovering truth is within the capacity of the youngest school-child. If you can get him to state candidly and without shame his doubtless erroneous ideas about the world, and give him leave to prove their correctness to you, you will have set in motion a process which is worthy to be called education; for it will constitute a genuine matching of theory with theory in his mind, a real training in inductive logic, and what conclusions he reaches will be truly his. When he sees in a familiar sunset, as he will see with a newly fascinated eye, the edge of the earth swinging up past the sun—then astronomy will be real to him, and full of meaning—and not a collection of dull facts that must be remembered against examination-day.

"This means that we must treat children as our equals. Education must embody a democratic relationship between adults and children. Children must be granted freedom of opinion—and freedom of opinion means nothing except the freedom to believe a wrong opinion until you are persuaded of a right one. They, moreover, must be the judges of what constitutes persuasion. You have asked me for practical and concrete suggestions in regard to education. I will make this one before I go: when I find an astronomy class in the first grade engaged in earnest debate as to whether the earth is round or flat, I will know that our school system has begun to be concerned for the first time with the inculcation of a love of truth. For, like Milton, I can not praise a fugitive and cloistered virtue, unexercised and unbreathed, that never sallies out and sees her adversary, but slinks out of the race, where that immortal garland is to be run for, not without dust and heat.—I thank you for your attention!"

XXII.
Enterprise.

AND so we come to Goodness—and at the same time to a change in our program. After calling on the Artist as an expert to testify in regard to Beauty, and the Philosopher to tell us about Truth, it would seem that we should hear about Goodness from a moralist. So, no doubt, you expected—and so I had originally intended. But it cannot have failed to secure your notice that our experts pursued a somewhat unconventional line of argument. The Artist told us that the way to teach children to love Beauty was to leave them free to hate it if they chose. The Philosopher said that the way to inculcate in children a love of Truth was to leave them free to hold wrong opinions. Now it is all very well to talk that way about Beauty and Truth. We might perhaps be persuaded to take such risks, so long as only Beauty and Truth were involved. But Goodness is a different matter. It simply would not do for us to hear any one who proposed a similar course in regard to conduct. Imagine any one suggesting that the way to teach children to be good is to leave them free to be bad! But that is just what I am afraid would happen if we called an expert on Morals to the stand. I have observed twenty or thirty of them shuffling their notes and their feet and waiting to be called on. But I do not trust them. No! Goodness is not going to be treated in so irreverent a fashion while I am running this discussion. I am going to see that this subject is treated with becoming reverence. And as the only way of making absolutely sure of this, I am going to address you myself.

We want children to grow up to be good men and women; and we want to know how the school can assist in this process. First, we must define goodness; and I shall suggest the rough outline of such a definition, which we must presently fill up in detail, by saying that goodness is living a really civilized life. And as one's conduct is not to be measured or judged except as it affects others, we may say that goodness is a matter of civilized relationships between persons. And furthermore, as the two most important things in life are its preservation and perpetuation, the two fields of conduct in which it is most necessary to be civilized are Work and Love. Let us first deal with Work and find out what constitutes civilized conduct in that field.

We all exist, as we are accustomed to remind ourselves, in a world where one must work in order to live. That, in a broad sense, is true; but there are certain classes of persons exempt from any such actual compulsion; and with respect to almost any specific individual outside of those classes, it is generally possible for him to escape from that compulsion if he chooses. Take any one of us here; you, for instance. If you really and truly did not want to work, you could find a way to avoid it; you could get your wife or your mother to support you by taking in washing or doing stenography—or, if they refused, you could manage to become the victim of some accident which would disable you from useful labor and enable you to spend your days peacefully in an institution. But you prefer to work; and the fact is that you like work. You are unhappy because you don't get a chance to do the work you could do best, or because you have not yet found the work you can do well; but you have energies which demand expression in work. And if you turn to the classes which are exempt from any compulsion to work, you find the rich expending their energies either in the same channels as everybody else, or organizing their play until its standards of effort are as exacting as those of work; you find women who are supported by their husbands rebelling against the imprisonment of the idle home, and seeking in all directions for employment of their energies; and as for the third class of those who do not have to work in order to live, we find that even idiots are happier when set at basket-weaving.

If we attempt to moralize upon the basis of these facts, we arrive at a conclusion something like this: it is right to use one's energies in organized effort—the more highly organized the better. And if we ask what is the impulse or trait or quality which makes people turn from an easy to a hard life, from loafing to sport, from sport to work, and which makes them contemptuous of each other and of themselves if they neglect an opportunity or evade a challenge to go into something still harder and more exacting—if we ask what it is that despite all our pretensions of laziness pushes us up more and more difficult paths of effort, we are obliged to call it Enterprise.

And when we face the fact that Enterprise is a love of difficulties for their own sake, we realize that the normal human being has, within certain limits, a pleasure in pain: for it is painful to run a race, to learn a language, to write a sonnet, to put through a deal—and pleasurable precisely because it is, within these limits, painful. If it is too easy, there is no fun in it. The extremer sorts of enterprise we call courage and heroism. But though we admire the fireman who risks his life in a burning building, we would not admire the man who deliberately set fire to his own bed in order to suffer the pangs of torture by fire; nor, although we admire the airmen who come down frozen from high altitudes, would we applaud a man who locked himself in a refrigerator over the week-end in order to suffer the torture of great cold. We would feel, in both these hypothetical cases, that there was no relevancy of their action to the world of reality. But upon this point our emotions are after all uncertain. We do not begrudge applause to the football-star who is carried from the field with a broken collar-bone, or to the movie-star who drives a motor-car off a cliff into the sea, though it is quite clear that these actions are relevant to and significant in the world of fantasy rather than the world of reality. What it comes down to is the intelligibility of the action. Does it relate to any world, of reality or of fantasy, which we can understand, which has any significance for us?

When we turn to the child, we find that normally he has no lack of enterprise. But his enterprise is relevant to a world of childish dreaming to which we have lost the key. His activities are largely meaningless to us—that is why we are so annoyed by them. And, in the same way, our kinds of enterprise are largely meaningless to him. That is why he usually objects so strongly to lessons and tasks. They interrupt and interfere with the conduct of his own affairs. He is as outraged at having to stop his play to put a shovelful of coal on the furnace, as a sober business man would be at being compelled, by some strange and tyrannical infantile despotism, to stop dictating letters and join, at some stated hour, in a game of ring-around-the-rosy. Most of what we object to as misconduct in children is a natural rebellion against the intrusion of an unimaginative adult despotism into their lives.

Nevertheless, it is our adult world that they are going to have to live in, and they must learn to live in it. And it is true, moreover, that much of their enterprise is capable of finding as satisfactory employment in what we term the world of reality as in their world of dreams. What we commonly do, however, is to convince them by punishment and scolding that our world of reality is unpleasant. What we ought to do is to make it more agreeable, more interesting, more fascinating, than their world of dreams. Our friend the Artist has already told us how this may be done, and our friend the Philosopher has given some oblique hints on the same subject. I merely note here that the school is the place in which the transition from the world of dreams to the world of realities may be best effected.

But there are various kinds of enterprise in our adult world. It is undoubtedly enterprising to hold up a pay-train, a la Jesse James. But though when the act involves real daring, we cannot withhold an instinctive admiration, yet we know that it is wrong. Why wrong? Because such acts disorganize and discourage, and if unchecked would ruin, the whole elaborate system of enterprise by which such trains are despatched and such money earned. It is obvious that train-robbery and wage-labor cannot fairly compete with one another; that if train-robbery goes on long enough, nobody will do wage-labor, and there will eventually cease to be pay-trains to rob. The law does not take cognizance of these reasons, but punishes train-robbery as a crime against property. Yet if we look into the matter for a moment, we realize that loyalty to any property system ultimately rests upon the conviction that its destruction would result in the total frustration of the finer sorts of human enterprise; it is for this reason that conservative people always persuade themselves that any change in the economic arrangements of society, from a new income-tax to communism, is a kind of train-robbery, bound to end in universal piracy and ruin. And this moral indignation, whether in any given instance appropriate or not—or whether, as in the case of many piratical kinds of business enterprise, left for long in abeyance—is the next step in our human morality. If we ask ourselves, why should not human enterprise turn into a welter of primitive piracy, with all the robbers robbing each other, we are compelled to answer that in the long run it would not be interesting. For, although destruction is temporarily more exciting, it is only construction that is permanently interesting. And if we ask why it is more interesting, we find that it is because it is harder. It is too easy to destroy. Destruction may be occasionally a good thing, as a tonic, something to give to individuals or populations a sense of power; but their most profound instinct is toward creation.

But the child, by reason of the primitive stage of his development, tends to engage rather more enthusiastically in destruction as a mode of enterprise than in creation. He tires of building, and it is a question whether or not the pleasure he takes in knocking over his houses of blocks does not exceed his pleasure in building them. He prefers playing at hunting and war to playing at keeping house. And his imagination responds more readily to the robber-exploits of Robin Hood than to the Stories of Great Inventors. This is a fact, but it need not discourage us. What is necessary is for him to learn the interestingness of creation. If what he builds is not a house of blocks on the nursery floor, but a wigwam in the woods, his destructive energies are likely to be satisfied in cutting down the saplings with which to build it. This simply means that his destructive energies have become subordinated to his constructive ones, as they are in adult life. But they cannot become so subordinated until what he constructs is wholly the result of his own wishes, and until moreover it is more desirable as the starting-point of new creative activities than as something to destroy. Those conditions are fulfilled whenever a group of children play together and have free access to the materials with which to construct. And that is what the school is for—to provide the materials, and the freedom, and be the home of a process by which children learn that it is more fun to create than to destroy.

XXIII.
Democracy.

BUT in our adult world, there is still another moral quality demanded of our human enterprise. It is not merely better to create than to destroy, but it is better to create something which is useful, or desirable, to others. Our moral attitude is a little uncertain upon this point, for the artist knows that his coarsest and easiest kind of enterprise is likely to be valued by others, and his finer and more difficult enterprises neglected and scorned. And so he has the impulse to work only for himself; nevertheless, he realizes that if he does work only for himself he is doing wrong. For he really feels a deep-lying moral obligation to work for others—a moral obligation which comes, of course, from his egoistic need of the spiritual sustenance of praise. The fact is that others are necessary to him, and that his work must please others. So if he ignores the crowd, it is because he wishes to compel it to take something better than what it asked for. And this democratic quality in enterprise becomes the third test of civilized life. Does a given action fit in everybody else's scheme as well as in your own: and, if it conflicts with the outside scheme, is it with a fundamentally altruistic intention? There are prophets and false prophets and of those who take the difficult course of disagreeing with their fellows, the best we can immediately demand of them is that they afflict us because they think it good for us and not because they do not care. Yet even so they differ from us at their peril. For we are to be the final judges of whether we are being imposed on or not. If we do not, after full consideration, feel that we can play our game if Napoleon or the Kaiser plays his, we put him out of business.

Now the child has a certain natural tendency toward the Napoleon-Kaiser attitude. He began, as we pointed out some time ago, by being an infantile emperor. He likes it. And being deposed by his parents does not alter his royalist convictions. For he has not merely been deposed—he has seen another king set up in his place. And one reason why parents are not the best persons to teach children democracy, is that they are the authors of the whole succession of enthronements and deposings which constitute the early history of a family. No, the children need a change of air—a chance to forget their Wars of the Roses and to take their places in a genuine democracy. The place for them to learn democracy (though I believe this has been said before) is the school. For in a properly conducted school there is an end of jealous little princes and princesses squabbling over prestige and appealing to the Power Behind the Throne; in such a school, conduct in general and work in particular is performed not with reference to such prestige as a reward, but with reference to their individual wishes in democratic composition with the wishes of their fellows.

But this will be true only if they find at school something different from what they have left at home. And what they have left at home may be described as a couple of well-meaning, bewildered and helpless people who are half the slaves of the children and half tyrants over them. It is unfortunate, but it is true, that the first that children learn of human relationships, is by personal experience of a relationship which is on both sides tyrannical and slavish. They naturally expect all their relationships with the adult world, if not with each other, to be conducted on this same pattern. They expect to find father and mother over again in the school-teacher. They hope to find the slave and fear to find the tyrant. But it is necessary that they should face the adult world into which they must grow up, as equals; and therefore they must begin to learn the lesson of equality. The school, by providing a kind of association between adults and children which is free from the emotional complexes of the home, can teach that lesson.

There is, however, so much intellectual confusion about what equality means that we must be quite clear on that point before we go on. At any moment of our careers, we are the servant of others, in the sense of being their follower, helper, disciple or right-hand man; and the master of still others, in that we are their leader, counsellor or teacher. We can hardly conduct an ordinary conversation without assuming, and usually shifting several times, these rôles. And these relationships extend far beyond the bounds of acquaintanceship, for one can scarcely read a book or write an article without creating such relationships for the moment with unknown individuals. In all the critical and important moments of one's life one is inevitably a leader or a follower. But in adult civilized life, these relationships are fluid; they change and exchange with each other. And they are fluid because they are free. You and I can choose, though perhaps not consciously, our leaders and our helpers; we are not condemned to stand in any fixed relationship to any other person. And this freedom to be servant of whom we please, and master of whom we can, is equality. If I want to know about fishing-tackle, I will sit at your feet and learn, and if you will condescend to lead the expedition in quest of these articles I will be your obedient follower; while if you happened to want advice about pens, pencils, ink, or typewriter-ribbons, you would, I trust, yield a similar deference to me. We have no shame in serving nor any egregious pride in directing each other, because we are equals. We are equals because we are free to become each other's master and each other's servant whenever we so desire.

But the relationship of parents and children is not free. Parents cannot choose their children, and must serve their helplessness willy-nilly. Children cannot choose their parents, and must obey them anyhow. It is a rare triumph of parenthood—and doubtless also of childhood—when children and parents become friends, and serve and obey each other not because they must but because they really like to. But schools can easily take up the task which parents are only with the greatest difficulty able to accomplish, and dissolve the infantile tyrant-and-slave relationship to the grown-up world. The grown-up people in the school can be the child's equals. They can become so by ceasing to encourage the notion which the child carries with him from the home, that adults are beings of a different caste. Once they regard an adult as a person like themselves—which, Heaven knows, he is!—children will discover quickly enough his admirable qualities, and his special abilities, and pay them the tribute of admiration and emulation. There is no human reason why a child should not admire and emulate his teacher's ability to do sums, rather than the village bum's ability to whittle sticks and smoke cigarettes; the reason why the child doesn't is plain enough—the bum has put himself on an equality with them and the teacher has not.

XXIV.
Responsibility.

BUT there is yet another quality which civilized standards demand of our human enterprise. People hate a quitter—and particularly the quitter whose defection leaves other people under the obligation to finish what he has started. We demand of a person that he should refrain from starting what he can't finish. This is a demand not only for democratic intentions, but for common sense and ordinary foresight. He shouldn't undertake a job that involves other people's putting their trust in him, unless he can really carry it through. And if he finds in the middle of it that he has, as the saying goes, "bit off more than he can chaw," he ought to try to stick it out at whatever cost to himself. If other people have believed he could do it, he must not betray their faith. This feeling is at the heart of what we ordinarily call telling the truth, as well as the foundation of the custom of paying one's debts. We don't really care how much a man perjures his own immortal soul by lying, but we do object to his fooling other people by it. We are all so entangled with each other, so dependent upon each other, that none of us can plan and create with any courage or confidence unless we can depend on others to do what they say they will do. But our feeling goes deeper than the spoken word—we want people to behave in accordance with the promise of their actions. We despise the person who seems, and who lets us believe that he is, wiser or more capable than he turns out to be. We even resent a story that promises at the beginning to be more interesting than it is when it gets going. And in regard to work, the thing which we value above any incidental brilliancy in its performance, is the certainty that it will be finished. Hence the pride in finishing any task, however disagreeable, once started.

This is the hardest thing that children have to learn—not to drop their work when they get tired of it. But it should be obvious that there is only one way for children to learn this, and that it is not by anything which may be said or done in punishment or rebuke from the authority which imposes the task. It is not to be learned at all so long as the task is imposed by any one outside the child himself. The child who is sent on an errand may forget, and not be ashamed. But the child who has volunteered to go on an errand—not as a pretty trick to please the Authorities, but because of a sense of the importance of the errand and of his own importance in doing it—that child has assumed a trust, which he will not be likely to violate.

But suppose, nevertheless, that he does forget. Here we come to the ethics of punishment—a savage ritual which we generally quite fail to understand. Let us take a specific case. A group of boys are building a house in the woods, and they run out of nails. Penrod says he will go home and get some from the tool-chest in the barn. He goes; and on the way, he meets a boy who offers to take him to the movies, where Charlie Chaplin is on exhibition. Penrod reflects upon his duty; but he says to himself that he will go in and see one reel of Charlie Chaplin, and then hurry away. But the inimitable Charles lulls him into forgetfulness of realities, and when he emerges from the theatre it is nigh on dinner time. Penrod realizes his predicament, and rehearses two or three fancy stories to account for his failure to return with the nails; but he realizes that none of them will hold. He wishes that a wagon would run over him and break his leg, so that he would have a valid excuse. But no such lucky accident occurs. How is he going to face the gang next day? He has set himself apart from them, exiled himself, by his act. The question is, how is he going to get back? Now in the psychology of children and savages, there is happily a means for such reinstatement. This means is the discharge of the emotions—in the offender and in the group against which he has offended—of shame on the one hand and anger on the other, which together constitute the barrier against his return. That is, if they can express their anger by, let us say, beating him up, that anger no longer exists, they are no longer offended. While if he can by suffering such punishment pay the debt of his offence, he thereby wipes it out of existence, and at the same time cleanses himself from the shame of committing it. As the best conclusion of an unpleasant incident, he is ready to offer himself for such punishment. For children understand the barbaric ritual of punishment when it really has the barbaric ritual significance.

But the punishment must be inflicted by the victim's peers. There are few adults who can with any dignity inflict punishment upon children—for the dignity with which punishment is given depends upon the equality of the punisher and the punished, and on the implicit understanding that if the case had happened to be different the rôles would have been reversed.

It will be perceived that this leaves discipline entirely a matter for children to attend to among themselves, with no interference by adults, and no imposition of codes of justice beyond their years and understanding. Punishment, in this sense, cannot be meted out unless the aggrieved parties are angry and the aggressor ashamed; but let no adult imagine that he can tell whether an offending child is ashamed or not. Shame is a destructive emotion which a healthy child tries to repress. He does not say, "I am sorry." He brazens out his crime until he provokes the injured parties to an anger which explodes into swift punishment, after which he is one of them again and all is well.

But the abdication of adults from the office of judge-jury-and-executioner of naughty children, destroys the last vestiges of the caste system which separates children from adults. It puts an end to superimposed authority, and to goodness as a conforming to the mysterious commands of such authority. It places the child in exactly such a relationship to a group of equals as he will bear in adult life, and it builds in him the sense of responsibility for his actions which is the final demand that civilization makes upon the individual. And the importance of the school as a milieu for such a process is in its opportunity to undo at once, early in life, the psychological mischief brought about, almost inevitably, by the influences of the home.

There!—I have let the cat out of the bag. I had intended to be very discreet, and say nothing that could possibly offend anybody. But I have said what will offend everybody—except parents. They, goodness knows, are fully aware that a home is no place to bring children up. They see what it does to the children plainly enough. But we, the children, are so full of repressed resentments against the tyrannies inflicted upon us by our parents, and so full of repressed shame at the slavery to which we subjected them, that we cannot bear to hear a word said against them. The sentimentality with which we regard the home is an exact measure of the secret grudge we actually bear against it. Woe to the person who is so rash as to say what we really feel!—But the mischief is done, and I may as well go on and say in plain terms that the function of the school is to liberate the children from the influences of parental love.

For parental love—as any parent will tell you—is a bond that constrains too tyrannically on both sides to permit of real friendship, which is a relationship between equals. The child goes to school in order to cease to be a son or daughter—and incidentally in order to permit the two harassed adults at home to cease in some measure to be father and mother. The child must become a free human being; and he can do so only if he finds in school, not a new flock of parents, but adults who can help him to learn the lesson of freedom and friendship. But that is something which I can discuss better in dealing with the subject of Love.

XXV.

Love.

REMEMBER that it is not my fault that we find ourselves discussing so inflammable a topic! But if you insist on knowing what education can do to bring our conduct in the realm of love up to the standard of civilization, I can but answer your question. We have found that in the realm of work, civilization demands of us Enterprise, and Democracy, and Responsibility. And I think that all the demands of civilization upon our conduct in the realm of love might be summed up in the same terms. We despise those persons who are afraid of adventure in love; who in devotion to some mawkish dream-ideal, turn away from the more difficult and poignant realities of courtship and marriage; and we are beginning to despise those whose enterprise is too cheaply satisfied in prostitution or in the undemocratic masculine exploitation of women of inferior economic status; and not only the crasser offences against sexual morality, but a thousand less definable but not less real offences within the realm of legal marriage, may be described as attempts to evade responsibility. I leave you to work out the implications of this system of morals for yourself. What I particularly want to speak of here is the effect of parental influences upon children with respect to their later love-life, and the function of education in dissolving those influences.

It is no secret that adults generally have not yet learned how to be happy in love. And the reason for that, aside from the economic obstacles to happiness which do not come within the scope of our inquiry, is that they are still children. They are seeking to renew in an adult relationship the bond which existed between themselves and their parents in infancy. Or they are seeking to settle a long-forgotten childish grudge against their parents, by assuming the parental rôle in this new relationship. And in both efforts, they find themselves encouraged by each other. Naturally enough! A woman likes to discover, and enjoys "mothering," the child in her husband; she likes to find also in him the god and hero which her father was to her in her infancy. And a happy marriage is one in which a man is at any moment unashamedly her child or (let us not shrink from using these infantile and romantic terms!) her god. But it is a bore to have to mother a man all the time; it is in fact slavery. And it is equally a bore to have to look up to a man all the time and think him wise and obey him; for that also is slavery. The happy marriage has something else—the capacity for swift and unconscious change and interchange of these rôles. The happy lovers can vary the tenor of their relationship because they are free to be more than one thing to each other. And they have that freedom because they are equals. That equality is comradeship, is friendship.

Do not imagine that friendship in love implies any absence of that profound worship and self-surrender which is characteristic of the types of love that are modelled upon the infantile and parental patterns. This is as ridiculous as it would be to suppose that equality in other fields of life means that no one shall ever lead and no one ever follow. Equality in love means only the freedom to experience all, instead of compulsion to experience only a part, of the emotional possibilities of love in a single relationship.

I would gladly explicate this aspect of my theme in some detail, were it not that it might incidentally comprise a catalogue of domestic difficulties and misunderstandings at once too tragic and too ridiculous—and some of you might object to my unfolding what you would consider to be your own unique and private woes in public.

I will, therefore, only point out that even what we term the civilized part of mankind is far from measuring up to this demand of civilization in the world of love, the demand for equality. It may seem somewhat of an impertinence to blame this fact upon the early influences of the home, when there are so many outstanding customs and laws and economic conditions which are founded on the theory of the inequality of men and women. But these customs and laws and conditions are in process of change—and the home influences of which I speak are not. Our problem is to consider if these influences may not be dissolved by the school. For, mark you, what happens when they are not! Wedded love, as based upon those undissolved influences, comes into a kind of disgrace; serious-minded men and women ask themselves whether such a bondage is tolerable; a thousand dramas and novels expose the iniquities of the thing; and the more intellectually adventurous in each generation begin to wonder if the attempt at faithful and permanent love ought not to be abandoned.

Let me relate only one widely typical—and perhaps only too-familiar—instance. A boy grows up poisoned with mother-love—er, I mean, petted and praised and waited upon by his mother, until he finds the outside world, with its comparative indifference to his wonderfulness, a very cold place indeed. Nevertheless, he adjusts himself to it, becomes a man, and falls in love. With whom does he fall in love? Perhaps with a girl like his mother; or perhaps with one quite opposite to her in all respects,—for he may have conceived an unconscious resentment against his mother, for betraying him by her praise into expecting too much of an unfeeling world. But in any case, he is going to experience again, in his relationship with his sweetheart, the ancient delights of being mothered. He is going to respond to that pleasure so unmistakably as to encourage the girl in further demonstrations of motherliness. He is in fact going to reward her more for motherliness than for any other trait in her possession. And the girl, who wants a lover and a husband and a man, is going to find herself with a child on her hands. But that is not the worst. If the girl does not rebel against the situation, the man is likely to, when he finds out just what it is. For he, too, despite his unconscious infantilism, wants a girl and a sweetheart and a wife. And when he realizes that he is being sealed up again in the over-close, over-sweet love-nest of his infancy, that he is becoming a baby, he revolts. He does not realize what has happened—he only knows that he no longer cherishes a romantic love for her. Naturally. Romantic love is a love between equals. She has become his mother—and he flees her, and perhaps goes through life seeking and escaping from his mother in half a hundred women. When this happens, we call him a Don Juan or a libertine or a scoundrel or a fool. But that does not alter his helplessness in the grip of infantile compulsions.

I do not wish to exaggerate the ability of education to dissolve, without the aid of a special psychic technique, any deeply-rooted infantile dispositions of this sort; but, aside from such flagrant cases, there are thousands of well-conducted men and women who just fail to free themselves sufficiently from the emotions of childhood to be happy in love. Besides their own selves, the sensible adult beings that they believe they are, there are within them pathetic and absurd children whose demands upon the relationship well-nigh tear it to pieces. It is in regard to these that it seems not improbable that a civilized education could secure their happiness for them. And it would do so by supplanting the emotionally over-laden atmosphere of the home with the invigorating air of equality. I refer in particular to equality between the sexes. So long as girls and boys are to any extent educated separately, encouraged to play separately, and treated as different kinds of beings, the remoteness hinders the growth of real friendship between the sexes, and leaves the mind empty of any realistic concepts which would serve to resist the transfer to the other sex, at the romantic age, of repressed infantile feelings about the beloved parent. What we have to deal with in children might without much exaggeration be described as the disinclination of one who has been a lover to become a friend. The emotions of the boy towards his mother are so rich and deep that he is inclined to scorn the tamer emotions of friendship with girl-children. (Notoriously, he falls in love first with older women in whom he finds some idealized image of his mother.) He is contemptuous of little girls because they are not the mother-goddess of his infancy. What he must learn, and the sooner the better, is that girls are interesting human beings, that they are good comrades and jolly playfellows. He must learn to like them for what they are. Ordinarily, the love-life of the adolescent boy is a series of more or less shocked discoveries that the women upon whom he has set his youthful fancy do not, in fact, correspond to his infantile dream. Half the difficulties of marriage are involved in the painful adjustment of the man to the human realities of his beloved; the other half being, of course, the similarly painful adjustment of the girl to similar human realities. He could be quite happy with her, were the other dear charmer, his infantile ideal, away. And it is one of the functions of education to chase this ideal away, to dissolve the early emotional bond to the parent, by making the real world in general and the real other sex in particular so *humanly* interesting that it will be preferred to the infantile fantasy.

I may be mistaken, but I think that half of this task will be easy enough. Girls, I am sure, are only in appearance and by way of saving their face, scornful of the activities of boys; they will be glad enough to join with them on terms of complete equality, and ready to admire and like them for what they humanly are. It will not be so easy to persuade boys to admire and like girls for what they are; and it will be the business of the school to dramatize unmistakably for these young masculine eyes the human interestingness of the other sex—to give the girls a chance to show their actual ability to compete on equal and non-romantic terms with boys in all their common undertakings.

To make realities more interesting than dreams—that is the task of education. And of all the realities whose values we ignore, in childish preoccupation with our feeble dreams, the human realities of companionship which each sex has to offer the other are among the richest. Despite all our romantic serenadings, men and women have only begun to discover each other. Just as, despite our solemn sermonizings on the blessedness of work, we have only begun to discover what creative activity can really mean to us. Work and love!—

A Voice. "Won't you please come back to the subject of education?"

What! Is it possible—is it credible—is it conceivable—that you have been following this discussion thus far, and have not yet realized that education includes everything on earth, and in the heavens above and the waters beneath? Come back to the subject of education! Why, it is impossible to wander away from the subject of education! I defy you to do so. All the books that have ever been written, all the pictures that have ever been painted, all the songs ever sung, all the machines ever invented, all the wars and all the governments, all the joyous and sorry loves of men and women, are but part of that vast process, the education of mankind. When you leave this discussion, you will not have dropped the subject; you will continue it in your next conversation, whether it be with your employer or your sweetheart or your milkman. You cannot get away from it. And though you perish, and an earthquake overwhelms your city in ruins, and the continent on which you live sinks in the sea, something that you have done or helped to do, something which has been a part of your life, the twisted fragments of the office building where you went to work or the old meerschaum pipe you so patiently coloured, will be dug up and gazed upon by future generations, and what you can teach them by these poor relics if by nothing else, will be a part of their education. . . .

XXVI.
Education in 1947 A. D.

BY way of epilogue, let us be Utopian, after the fashion of Plato and H. G. Wells. Let me, as a returned traveller from the not-too-distant future, picture for you concretely the vaster implications of education in, say, the year 1947, as illustrated by the public school in the village of Pershing, N. Y.

* * * * *

"But which is the school-building?" I asked my guide.

He laughed. "I am surprised at you," he said. "Surprised that you should ask such a question!"

"Why?" I demanded innocently.

"Because," he said, "in the files of our historical research department I once came across a faded copy of a quaint old war-time publication called the *Liberator*.[4] It attracted my attention because it appeared to have been edited by a grizzled old fire-eater whom I recently met, Major General Eastman, the head of our War College. In those days, it seems, he thought he was a pacifist. Time's changes!"

"Ah, yes—General Eastman. I remember him well," I said. "But what has that got to do with—"

"In that curious little magazine was an article on education. It was signed by you. Don't you remember what you wrote? Didn't you believe what you said? Or didn't you fully realize that you were living in a time when prophecies come true? You ask me where the school-building is. Why, there isn't any school-building."

We were standing in the midst of a little park, about the size of a large city block, bordered by a theatre, a restaurant, an office-building, several handsome factory buildings of the newer and more cheerful style, a library, a newspaper plant, and a church.

My companion pointed to one of the buildings. "That," he said, "is the children's theatre. There they present their own plays and pageants. In connection

[4] In which some of these chapters originally appeared, and to which my thanks are due for the privilege of republication.

with the work there they learn singing and dancing, scene painting, and costume. Of course they also learn about plays—I suppose from your primitive point of view you would say that we conduct a course in dramatic literature. But all those antique phrases of early educational practice have passed out of use. We would say that the children are learning to develop their creative impulses. We consider our theatre very important in that respect. It is the beginning of everything.

"Next in importance, perhaps, are those factories. They include a carpenter shop, a pottery, and a machine shop. Here is made everything which is used throughout the school. And there is the power house which furnishes the electric current for the whole establishment. You understand, of course, that the boys and girls get a complete theoretical as well as practical grasp of the facts they are dealing with—there is no neglect of what I suppose you would call book-learning, here.

"Over there is the textile and garment factory, which designs and makes the costumes for the plays and pageants. You will not be surprised to learn that the garment-makers at any given period are the most active supporters of the propaganda for an outdoor theatre. It would give them a chance to do more costumes!...

"Yes, we have politics here. The question of an outdoor theatre is being agitated very warmly just now. The pupils have complete control of the school budget of expenditure. There is only so much money to spend each year, you see, at present, though there is a movement on foot to make the institution self-supporting; but I'm afraid that will depend on the political situation. Ultimately, of course, we expect to put the whole of industry under the Department of Education. . . . But I'm afraid that's going too deeply into a situation you could hardly be expected to understand.

"At any rate to return to our school, the opposition to the outdoor theatre is from the scientific groups, who want an enlargement of their laboratories. . . . The architectural and building groups are neutral—they are working on plans for both projects, and all they want is that the question should be settled one way or the other at once, so they can go to work. There will be a meeting tonight, at which a preliminary vote will be taken. Yes, our politics are quite old-fashioned—Greek, in fact.

"The shops? They are managed by shop committees of the workers. Distribution of products to the various groups which use them is effected through a distributing bureau, which has charge of the book-keeping and so forth. There has been a change in distribution recently, however. At first the shops merely made what was ordered by the various groups, and requisitions were the medium of exchange. But the shops became experimental and enterprising, and produced what they liked on the chance of its being wanted. This made a show-place necessary, and as for various reasons ordinary money became the medium of exchange, the show-place became a kind of department store. Then some of the groups decided to use part of their subsidy in advertising in the school newspaper and magazines. They are working out some very interesting principles in their advertising, too, as you will find. They have to tell the truth. . . .

"There is the printing establishment. No, the paper and the magazines are not self-supporting—though the school advertising helps. They're subsidized. We quite believe in that.

"And there—you can get a glimpse of the greenhouses and gardens. Botany and so forth. . . . The library is the centre of the research groups. History, sociology, economics—finding out what and why. Very informal and very earnest, as you'll find. . . . The groups? Oh, the time one stays in each group varies with the individual. But every one likes to be able to boast quietly of an M. P.—that means a 'masterpiece' in the old mediaeval sense; a piece of work that shows you've passed the apprentice stage—in a reasonable number of departments. Some Admirable Crichtons go in for an M. P. in everything!. . .

"The restaurant—that's quite important. The cooking groups give a grand dinner every little while, and everybody goes and dines quite in state, with dancing afterward. We learn the best of bourgeois manners—makes it *quite* impossible to distinguish an immigrant's child from the scions of our old families. The result is that the best families are discarding their manners in order to retain their distinction! Very amusing. . . .

"The church? You mean that building over there, I suppose? That isn't a church—not in the sense you mean. It's our meeting place. You see, since your time churches have come to be used so much for meetings that when our architecture group came to plan an assembly hall it was quite natural for them to choose the ecclesiastical style. Anyway, I understand it's a return to their original purpose. . . ."

"But," I said, "this school is just like the world outside!"

"Except," he said, "in one particular. In the world outside we still have certain vestiges of class privilege and exploitation—considerably toned down from their former asperities, but still recognizable as relics of capitalism. In the school we have play, production and exchange as they would exist in the outside world if these things were to be done and managed wholly with the intention of making better and wiser and happier citizens. The difference, of course, is simply that one is run with an educational and the other with a productive intention."

"The difference seems to me," I remarked, "that your school is really democratic and your adult world isn't quite."

"That is one way of putting it," he conceded.

"And I should think," I said warmly, "that after going to these schools, your people would want the rest of the world run on exactly the same plan."

"It does rather have that effect," he admitted cautiously. "In fact, the Educational party, as it is called, is very rapidly rising into power. Since you are unfamiliar with our politics, I should explain that the Educational party was formed, after the unfortunate events of 1925, by the amalgamation of the United Engineers, the O. G. U., and the Farmers' League. Its chief figure is the sainted Madame Goldman, the organizer of the Women's Battalion in the First Colonial War. . . ."

"What surprises me," I interrupted, "is that your conservatives—"

"Tut! we have no conservatives—they call themselves Moderates."

"I am surprised, then, that your Moderates allow such schools to exist! Of course they will revolutionize any society in which they are!"

"Well," said my companion, "but what could they do? Once you begin making schools *for* the children, you start out on the principle that education is learning how to live—and you end here."

I pondered this. "Not necessarily," I said at last. "You might have ended with schools in which the children of the poor were taught how to be efficient wage-slaves."

"Ah, yes," said my friend, "but they smashed that attempt away back in 1924."

"Did they? I'm very glad to hear it!" I cried. . . . "By the bye, how much do these schools cost—all over the country?"

"Less per year than we spent per day on the Second Colonial War. . . . But this is enough of description. You shall see for yourself. Come!" he said.

We started toward the theatre.

"Play," he was saying, "is according to our ideas more fundamental and more important in life than work. Consequently the theatre—"

But what he said about the theatre would take us far from anything which we are now accustomed to consider education. It involves no less a heresy than the calm assumption that the artist type is the highest human type, and that the chief service which education can perform for the future is the deliberate cultivation of the faculty of "creative dreaming." . . .

I venture to quote only one sentence:

"Mankind needs more poets."

Appendix.

A Definition of Progressive Education.

(From a bulletin issued by the Progressive Education Association, Washington, D. C.)

"The aim of Progressive Education is the freest and fullest development of the individual, based upon the scientific study of his physical, mental, spiritual, and social characteristics and needs.

"Progressive Education as thus defined implies the following conditions:

"1. Freedom To Develop Naturally

"The conduct of the pupil should be self-governed according to the social needs of his community, rather than by arbitrary laws. . . . Full opportunity for initiative and self-expression should be provided, together with an environment rich in interesting material that is available for the free use of every pupil.

"2. Interest the Motive of All Work

"Interest should be satisfied and developed through: (1) Direct and indirect contact with the world and its activities, and use of the experience thus gained. (2) Application of knowledge gained, and correlation between different subjects. (3) The consciousness of achievement.

"3. The Teacher a Guide, Not a Task-Master

". . . Progressive teachers will encourage the use of all the senses, training the pupils in both observation and judgment; and instead of hearing recitations only, will spend most of the time teaching how to use various sources of information, including life activities as well as books; how to reason about the information thus acquired; and how to express forcefully and logically the conclusions reached. Teachers will inspire a desire for knowledge, and will serve as guides in the investigations undertaken, rather than as task-masters. To be a proper inspiration to their pupils, teachers must have ample opportunity and encouragement for self-improvement and for the development of broad interests.

"4. Scientific Study of Pupil Development

"School records should . . . include both objective and subjective reports on those physical, mental, moral, and social characteristics which affect both school and adult life, and which can be influenced by the school and the home. Such records should be used as a guide for the treatment of each pupil, and should also serve to focus the attention of the teacher on the all-important work of development, rather than on simply teaching subject matter.

"5. Greater Attention to All that Affects the Child's Physical Development

"One of the first considerations of Progressive Education is the health of the pupils. Much more room in which to move about, better light and air, clean and well ventilated buildings, easier access to the out of doors and greater use of it, are all necessary. There should be frequent use of adequate playgrounds. . . .

"6. Co-operation Between School and Home to Meet the Needs of Child-Life

"The school should provide, with the home, as much as possible of all that the natural interests and activities of the child demand, especially during the elementary school years. It should give opportunity for manual experience for both boys and girls, for home-making, and for healthful recreation of various kinds. . . . These conditions can come about only through intelligent co-operation between parents and teachers. It is the duty of the parents to know what the school is doing and why. . . .

"7. The Progressive School a Leader in Educational Movements

"The Progressive School should be . . . a laboratory where new ideas if worthy meet encouragement; where tradition alone does not rule, but the best of the past is leavened with the discoveries of today, and the result is freely added to the sum of educational knowledge.

"*(The Association is not committed, and never can be, to any particular method or system of education. In regard to such matters it is simply a medium through which improvements and developments worked out by various agencies can be presented to the public.)*"

Printed by Libri Plureos GmbH in Hamburg,
Germany